T0036071

THE BOOK OF
JAPANESE FOLKLORE

An Encyclopedia of the Spirits, Monsters, and Yōkai of Japanese Myth

The Stories of the Mischievous Kappa, Trickster Kitsune, Horrendous Oni, and More

Thersa Matsuura
Creator of the *Uncanny Japan* Podcast

Illustrated by Michelle Wang

ADAMS MEDIA
NEW YORK   LONDON   TORONTO   SYDNEY   NEW DELHI

Adams Media
An Imprint of Simon & Schuster, LLC
100 Technology Center Drive
Stoughton, Massachusetts 02072

Copyright © 2024 by Thersa Matsuura.

All rights reserved, including the right
to reproduce this book or portions
thereof in any form whatsoever. For
information, address Adams Media
Subsidiary Rights Department, 1230
Avenue of the Americas, New York, NY
10020.

First Adams Media hardcover edition
April 2024

ADAMS MEDIA and colophon are
registered trademarks of Simon &
Schuster, LLC.

Simon & Schuster: Celebrating 100
Years of Publishing in 2024

For information about special
discounts for bulk purchases,
please contact Simon & Schuster
Special Sales at 1-866-506-1949 or
business@simonandschuster.com.

The Simon & Schuster Speakers Bureau
can bring authors to your live event. For
more information or to book an event,
contact the Simon & Schuster Speakers
Bureau at 1-866-248-3049 or visit our
website at www.simonspeakers.com.

Interior design by Kellie Emery
Interior images © 123RF/chatree
jiamwattanasuk
Illustrations by Michelle Wang

Manufactured in China

10 9 8 7 6 5 4 3 2 1

Library of Congress Cataloging-in-
Publication Data
Names: Matsuura, Thersa, author. |
Wang, Michelle, illustrator.
Title: The book of Japanese folklore
/ Thersa Matsuura, creator of the
Uncanny Japan podcast; illustrated by
Michelle Wang.
Description: First Adams Media
hardcover edition. | Stoughton,
Massachusetts: Adams Media, [2024] |
Series: World mythology and folklore |
Includes index.
Identifiers: LCCN 2023037723 |
ISBN 9781507221914 (hc) | ISBN
9781507221921 (ebook)
Subjects: LCSH:
Folklore--Japan--Encyclopedias.
Classification: LCC GR340 .M384 2024 |
DDC 398.20952--dc23/eng/20231011
LC record available at https://
lccn.loc.gov/2023037723

ISBN 978-1-5072-2191-4
ISBN 978-1-5072-2192-1 (ebook)

Many of the designations used
by manufacturers and sellers to
distinguish their products are
claimed as trademarks. Where those
designations appear in this book and
Simon & Schuster, LLC, was aware of a
trademark claim, the designations have
been printed with initial capital letters.

DEDICATION

To Rich Pav,

For saving me, rooting for me, and making every single day an absolute joy. Without you, none of this would have been possible.

CONTENTS

Preface 8

Introduction 10

Japanese Culture and Folklore 13

ABE NO SEIMEI: Legendary Astrologer and Mystic 19

AKANAME: The Filth Licker. 25

AMABIE: A Prophetic Sea Creature 28

AZUKIARAI: The Red Bean Washer. 34

BAKENEKO AND NEKOMATA: Monster Cats. 39

BAKU: The Dream Eater 43

BINBŌGAMI: The Poverty God 49

DOROTABŌ: The Muddy Rice Field Man. 53

FUTAKUCHI ONNA: The Two-Mouthed Woman 59

HASHIHIME: The Bridge Princess 65

HITOTSUME KOZŌ: The One-Eyed Boy 69

ITTAN MOMEN: The Bolt of Cotton. 74

JINMENJU, JINMENKEN, AND JINMENGYO:
The Human-Faced Tree, Dog, and Fish. 78

JINMENSŌ: The Human-Faced "Tumor" 82

JORŌGUMO: The Harlot Spider 87

KAMAITACHI: The Sickle Weasel 91

KAPPA: The River Child or Water Goblin 95

KINTARŌ: The Golden Boy 101

KITSUNE: The Fox 105

KODAMA: The Tree Spirit 111

KONAKI JIJI: The Old Man Who Cries Like a Baby 115

MOMOTARŌ: The Peach Boy 119

NINGYO: Mermaids 125

NOPPERABŌ: The No-Faced Creature 129

NUE: The Dreadful Chimeric Beast 135

ŌKAMI: The Wolf 139

ONI: Ogres or Demons 145

ONIBI AND KITSUNEBI: Demon Fires and Fox Fires 150

RAIJIN AND FŪJIN: The God of Thunder and Storms
and the God of Wind 155

RAIJŪ: The Thunder Beast 159

ROKUROKUBI: The Long-Necked Woman 163

RYŪ: Dragons 167

TANUKI: The Racoon Dog 173

TENGU: The Mountain Goblin 177

TŌFU KOZŌ: The Tofu Boy 183

TSUCHIGUMO: The Earth Spider 187

TSUCHINOKO: The Child-of-Hammer Snake 191

TSUKUMOGAMI: Haunted Artifacts 197

UMIBŌZU: The Sea Monk 200

URASHIMA TARŌ: The Fisher Lad 203

USHIONI: The Ox Demon 207

YAMAUBA: The Mountain Witch 213

YATAGARASU: The Three-Legged Crow 218

YUKI ONNA: The Snow Woman 221

ZASHIKI WARASHI: The Parlor-Room Child 227

Further Reading 230

Glossary 232

Index 236

ACKNOWLEDGMENTS

I'd like to express my heartfelt appreciation and love to my friends, family, patrons, and those who have supported me and all my quirky creative endeavors. I could have done none of this without you. Your wise insights, encouragement, and belief in me throughout the years, and while writing this book, have kept me going and kept me sane. Thank you for everything.

Paul Biba, Gina Carter, Daniel Cook, Thomas and Peggy Czechowski, David Dastmalchian, Ethan Ellenberg (agent extraordinaire), Eric Gage, Erik Howden, Keiko Iijima, Pamela Jewel, Yukiko Kawabata, Michelle Knopf, Yoshio Kuboyama, Linda Lombardi, Luca, Karen Masuda, Julyan Ray Matsuura, Kōitsu and Sanae Matsuura, Motoki and Mikito Matsuura, Joanna Matsunaga, Chris McClory, Andy McLellan, Priya Monrad, Susie and Steve Molnar, Amoretta Morris, Miwa Nito, Gabriel Novo, Yuki Otsuka, Evan J. Peterson, Rich Pav, Doris Pavonarius, Dollar Rain, Dennis Faxholm Rasmussen, Steven Redford, John H. Roberts, Kaho Saito, Gina Schwaderer, Michelle Shene, Courtney Ellis Smith, Erika Sone, Kazumi Sone, Leah Strebin, Sue Sullivan, Patty Suzuki, Jean Taylor, Jas Todd, Steve Urick, Dan Watson, Annette "Boss" Wilkinson, Mari Yagi, Mélissa Yoyotte, and my entire Clarion West family.

PREFACE

After a childhood living all over the US—as far north as Fairbanks, Alaska, and as far south as Jacksonville, Florida—I ended up heading east, Far East. I first came to Japan in 1990 on a Japanese Ministry of Education Scholarship. I studied the language at Shizuoka University for two years, then decided to live here permanently. I married a Japanese man and started a family.

I immediately fell in love with Japan—the language, the culture, the people, and all the unique folklore, superstitions, and multitudes of strange beasties that seemed to be lurking everywhere. I wanted to learn more about this mysterious and fascinating country. The early nineties was a time before widespread Internet, so my research was all very hands-on; I'd check out books from the local library and translate them, or would sit on a tatami mat floor with my Japanese friends and relatives as we conversed over a cup of green tea.

While exciting, living in a foreign country is also isolating at times. Back then, there were no fellow English speakers in my small town, and international phone calls were short, expensive, and could only be made once a month from a special phone booth that was a twenty-minute walk away.

Plus, I had a very superstitious mother-in-law who was convinced I attracted ghosts and various spirits that liked to stick to me and cause bad things to happen. This was a daily reminder of how much I still didn't understand about the culture. To cope and survive this difficult time, I decided to open my mind more, do additional research, and try to understand why such superstitions came about. Then I'd write stories to share my experiences with others.

I ended up writing a couple of books—a story collection in a genre I call "mythical realism" titled *A Robe of Feathers and Other Stories,* and a second one in the horror genre called *The Carp-Faced Boy and Other Tales.* In late 2016, I also started my bimonthly podcast, *Uncanny Japan.* In it, I share all the strange legends, curious cultural tidbits, and obscure folklore I dig up when doing research for my writing.

As you can see, the characters highlighted in this book have become an everyday part of my life. I hope you are as fascinated by this one-of-a-kind folklore pantheon as I am.

—Thersa

INTRODUCTION

- A fox called a kitsune suddenly transforms into an enchanting, kimono-wearing woman.

- A giant red-skinned, ogreish oni stomps onto your path, raises its spiked iron club, and roars.

- The amabie, a bird-beaked sea creature, bobs off the coast, warning people of an upcoming pandemic.

These are only a few of the innumerable wonderfully weird and wildly entertaining mythical creatures that have been inhabiting Japan for more than two thousand years. First written about in the ancient chronicles the *Kojiki* (C.E. 712) and *Nihon Shoki* (C.E. 720), these tales have been passed down from generation to generation, adapted, embellished, and added to through written records, oral storytelling, artwork, poetry, and plays. Some stories were even reported as true happenings in early news periodicals called kawaraban.

Given Japan's long history and its people's rich imaginations, it's no wonder this small island nation is home to so many gods (kami), spirits, monsters, folk heroes, and villains—as well as all manner of uniquely Japanese supernatural beasties called yōkai. For the most part, all of these otherworldly beings stayed safely inside Japan's borders until the Internet became widely available and they spread worldwide. Multilayered beasties that range from the heroic to the savage and from the silly to the seductive and every combination in between left Japan to frighten, mystify, and charm people all over the world. Today, you can find them in popular comics, manga, anime, movies, and games.

The dozens of entries in *The Book of Japanese Folklore* will introduce you to a good many of these characters and give you some insight into who they are, what they do, where they came from, and what their place is in Japanese history and culture. You'll learn the various ways they've evolved over time, some of their more interesting quirks, any well-known story they're involved in, and where you might have bumped into them in recent times.

Whether you're familiar with any of these characters or are meeting them all for the first time, you're sure to be entertained, enlightened, and surprised by these uncanny individuals and their stories. Get ready to meet quirky animals, wise elders, and peculiar shape-shifters—you'll never see the world quite the same way again!

JAPANESE CULTURE AND FOLKLORE

The Power and Mystery of Japanese Folklore

Japan has a rich history that has always been wonderfully interwoven with spectacular legends, timeless tales, and otherworldly creatures. What's both fascinating and surprising, though, is that this history is not so far removed from the present day. Even now, the line that separates hard reality from the supernatural and the fanciful is not as distinct as you might think.

For example, a person's extended bout of bad luck might be blamed on a run-in with the binbōgami, or poverty god. On the other hand, a sudden influx of fortune—be it monetary or the good luck of meeting your perfect partner—could have come about because you were visited one night by a lucky ghostly child called a zashiki warashi. House builders still take care not to place windows, doors, stoves, or toilets in the northeastern section of a home. This area is called a kimon, or demon's gate, and devious oni (ogre-type beasts) can enter from here, bringing with them mayhem and misfortune. (The best thing to place in the kimon area, by the way, is a closet or wall.) In your yard, a prickly holly bush will keep those pesky demons away.

Anyone who has studied, visited, or lived in Japan can surely agree that this is a country that recognizes, honors, celebrates—and oftentimes fears—the unseen parts of daily life. All the deities, creatures, and spirits that lurk in those hidden places feel very real indeed.

Understanding the Terminology and Origins of Folklore

Throughout history, the entities mentioned in Japanese folklore have gone by a lot of different names, such as: *mononoke, ayakashi, obake, bakemono, henge, yūrei, kami,* and *yōkai.* Some of these terms aren't used very often today, so let's look at the two you will most likely encounter.

The first one is *kami* (神). It's translated in English as "god," but the meaning is much broader than a sacred, all-powerful deity. Per Shinto belief, kami are spirits or divine forces that can be found in all things in nature, and yet they can also move around at will, even inhabiting people. Despite being labeled "gods," they aren't all benign do-gooders. Some kami are more sinister, even wrathful, causing ill fortune, disease, or chaos. Examples include the hōsōgami (god of smallpox) or binbōgami (god of poverty).

The second word that you'll hear quite a bit is *yōkai* (妖怪). Recently, when I was talking with a friend about Japanese creation myths and how to distinguish between these different categories, he said it was easy: "The gods made us, but we made yōkai." Yōkai are believed to have come from ancient humans' fear and awe of their surroundings. Each creature that was creatively whispered about and drawn into life filled a need to understand something beyond comprehension. Life outside (and, at times, inside) the house could be scary. Think of sudden diseases sweeping into a community, natural disasters, and bizarre and dangerous animals that lived in the forests, mountains, or oceans. Ancient people used yōkai as one way to make sense of it all.

For example, the rare and shocking occurrence of what we now know as ball lightning was rumored to be an overly excited, destructive yōkai called a raijū (thunder beast), which descended during storms and started darting about obnoxiously. Or if someone came across an unexplained rattling noise echoing throughout the hills while hiking alone, they might very well explain it as an azukiarai, a mysterious bean washer, vigorously rinsing his beans in a wooden bowl by the riverbank.

These yōkai appear in the earliest historical Japanese texts, scrolls, and art, existing in the liminal spaces throughout the ages: in the day's dying light, on bridges or crossroads, in abandoned temples, or in the quiet, deep parts of rivers. They can be nightmarish, ridiculous, or enchanting. While reading the following entries, I'm sure you'll find (more than once) that people's imaginations were exceptional and unique.

Overlapping Stories

For over a thousand years, the Shinto and Buddhist religions have existed in Japan next to a plethora of legends, superstitions, and folk beliefs. Because of this, the stories found in belief systems often intertwined with folkloric and supernatural tales, causing them to merge and evolve in incredible ways.

Are these creatures mythical monsters, spirits, ghosts, or folkloric heroes? The answer is, they can be all of them at once! Consider, for example, the story of a popular folk hero from a children's fairy tale, Kintarō. Kintarō was a boy born to a mountain witch after she was impregnated by a thunderclap. As a youth, his exploits included wrestling and defeating bears, but then he grew up and met a famed, real-life hero and samurai named Minamoto no Yorimitsu.

Minamoto no Yorimitsu was putting together a powerful and loyal team he dubbed the Shitennō, or Four Heavenly Kings. The name derives from a Buddhist term that describes four celestial guardians and protectors who also just happen to look like fierce warriors. After Kintarō met with Minamoto no Yorimitsu, the child hero changed his name to Sakata no Kintoki and joined the Four Heavenly Kings. Together, they battled (and defeated) the most heinous oni ogre in all of Japan, Shuten Dōji, as well as the giant yōkai spider monster, the tsuchigumo, or dirt spider.

Kintarō is therefore a folktale character who grew up to become an actual famous samurai, defeating dreadful mythical creatures, then dying the death of a man. He was eventually enshrined in at least one place (Kintoki Jinja), and parents wishing for their sons to grow up healthy and strong, just like the folk hero, pray to him there as a kami god.

So, as you can see, creatures can fall under more than one category. You'll find both Buddhism and the Shinto belief system are often intertwined with folklore and supernatural creatures. When studying Japanese folklore, it is best to keep an open mind and be watchful for the connections, since the supernatural and mythical will often entwine with the real and historically accurate.

Common Sources

In *The Book of Japanese Folklore*, you'll find background information that explains these creatures for people who are completely new to Japanese folklore—but there are also interesting insights and little-known theories for those who are more knowledgeable about the subject. As thorough as this book is, it is by no means the last word on any of these tales or the characters in them. Every one of them has centuries of retellings and reimaginings, different interpretations, as well as thousands of local variations that both deepen and color their legends to make them even more unique.

I'd also like to encourage you to look at a map or search online when specific places, temples, shrines, cities, or prefectures (which are defined districts or regions) are mentioned throughout the text. There is remarkable diversity in traditions and ways of storytelling all over Japan, and it's fascinating to see how that influences and colors the tales. As for more modern pop culture references, I touched on a few in each entry, but it would be impossible to list every place one of these beasties appeared. Please feel free to use the book as a jumping-off point to seek out even more of them!

Two of the most important sources worth noting are the *Kojiki* (古事記), or *The Record of Ancient Matters*, and the *Nihon Shoki* (日本書紀), or *The*

Chronicles of Japan. Together they are heralded as the most important historical texts in Japan, giving valuable insight into early history, mythology, and culture. The *Kojiki* is the older of the two, compiled in C.E. 712. It was commissioned by Empress Genmei and completed by Ō no Yasumaro. It mixed historical events with myths and legends. The *Nihon Shoki* (also called the *Nihongi*) was put together in C.E. 720 and gives a more detailed account of everything from the mythological beginnings of Japan to the genealogy of the emperors, to the mention of what would become the folk hero Urashima Tarō, who you'll read about later.

A third important source often mentioned is *Gazu Hyakki Yagyō* (画図百鬼夜行), or *Illustrated Demon Horde's Night Parade* (1776), and the three volumes that followed. These four books, written by Toriyama Sekien (1712–1788), are each a collection of woodblock prints that include a brief story or explanation of the various yōkai, monsters, and other supernatural creatures. The series includes a mix of both creatures that were already well known at the time and completely original yōkai, imagined in Sekien's brilliant and hilarious mind.

These images and bits of stories, as well as other ancient scrolls and woodblock print books, are the basis for most of the yōkai you see and hear about today. Some more of my favorite sources are listed in the back of this book.

The Yōkai and You

The stories of these otherworldly creatures have prevailed in Japan throughout the centuries for a reason. Whether it's for entertainment and escape, or for more noble causes—to illuminate different ways of thinking and living, offer comfort in the face of the incomprehensible, or provide insight into the human psyche—these beloved and powerful forces in Japanese culture are finally making their way around the world to startle, frighten, educate, and woo.

If you'd like to read more about specific stories and creatures that have piqued your curiosity, or if you're interested in learning about the legends as a whole, *The Book of Japanese Folklore* is here to shine a light on these extraordinary tales, illuminating the shadowy places these bizarre and wonderful creatures reside. Remember to keep your eyes and mind open too, because this is just the beginning. In Japan there is a saying, "Yaoyorozu no kami," which translates to something like, "Japan is a country with eight million gods or spirits." But "eight million" actually alludes to an infinite number. There are a lot more where these came from!

ABE NO SEIMEI

安倍晴明

Pronunciation: AH-beh no SAY-meh

Also known as: The Merlin of Japan

Overview

Abe no Seimei (C.E. 921–1005) was an actual historical person but also what you might today call a powerful "high wizard." Proof of his existence comes from the voluminous literature written about him while he was alive, as well as the books he compiled and authored himself, such as *Senji Ryakketsu* (占事略決), which is filled with a multitude of detailed techniques about everything from bringing about much-needed rain to conjuring lethal curses.

He spent most of his life working for the government, emperors, and the Heian imperial court (the ruling leadership from C.E. 794–1185) as a specialist in divination and magic, sometimes performing truly extraordinary feats. Abe no Seimei was adept in the practice of Onmyōdō (陰陽道), or the Way of Yin and Yang. Onmyōdō was an eclectic system that, while developed in Japan, mixed together various Chinese and Japanese practices and philosophies, such as the Theory of the Five Elements (wood, fire, earth, metal, water), Taoism, Buddhism, Confucianism, and Shintoism. Combine all that with a dash of fox magic, and you get a unique and powerful supernatural system called Onmyōdō. A person who practiced this was called an onmyōji (陰陽師), and undoubtedly, the most famous onmyōji was Abe no Seimei.

To say Abe no Seimei's duties as an onmyōji were diverse would be an understatement. On any given day, he could be asked to predict the outcome of a battle, locate the best place to dig a well, find hidden or lost objects (or people, for that matter), predict the sex of an unborn child, make a calendar, create a magical protection charm, determine both lucky and unlucky days for an upcoming event, help decide where to put a new building, give advice on military strategy, or exorcise a demon.

Abe no Seimei was able to accomplish all of this by using his versatile skill set of meditation, astrology, cosmology, geomancy, meteorology, chrononomy, divination, reading omens, as well as his gift for being able to commune with gods (kami), spirits of the dead, yōkai, and even demons—especially minor servant spirits called shikigami (式神), which he could coerce into doing his bidding. The practice of Onmyōdō was completely banned in 1870.

Background and Popular Stories

Because Abe no Seimei's mastery of Onmyōdō was so heralded and unmatched in his day, when the great mystical hero passed away (in the year 1005, at the remarkable, ripe old age of eighty-four), word of his stellar reputation spread throughout Japan, and awe led to exaggeration. "Abe the person" quickly turned into "Abe the magical superhero" of myth and legend. These lines are blurred to such an extent that it is sometimes difficult to separate fact from fiction. But if you want to try, many legends are collected in a book called *Konjaku Monogatarishū* (今昔物語種), or *An Anthology of Past Tales*, and there are many fascinating accounts of his life.

One interesting story involves Abe no Seimei's rival, a fellow onmyōji named Ashiya Dōman, aptly nicknamed "The Evil Dōman." (Compare that moniker to Abe no Seimei's, which was "Seimei of Justice.") One of their best-known duels took place when Abe no Seimei was still quite young. The sneaky Dōman challenged the youthful Abe to compete against him in divining what was inside a sealed box. Abe no Seimei agreed. Ashiya Dōman deviously conspired to have fifteen mikan oranges placed inside the box before the event.

When the day arrived, Ashiya Dōman confidently prognosticated in front of the court and an enthralled audience that there were fifteen mikans in the box. Now, Abe no Seimei might have been young, but he wasn't born yesterday. He used his own preternatural powers to see through Dōman's trick. But instead of calling him out on the ruse, the young "Seimei of Justice" announced that, no, there were actually fifteen rats inside the box. Imagine Dōman's surprise when the box was unsealed and out scurried a swarm of furry rodents. Ashiya Dōman was not only shocked; he was defeated.

Abe no Seimei also used a super-powerful (and super-secret) spell called Taizan Fukun no Sai (泰山府君祭). It translates as the "Lord Taizan Ceremony," which might sound boring until you realize that Lord Taizan is the god of a mountain in China (Taishan) and also one of the kings of hell. The spell could be used to lengthen someone's life, save someone from death, or (if you were really lucky) bring someone back from the dead. Abe no Seimei and his clan were the only ones who knew the exact details on how to perform this highly coveted, inconceivable wicked magic. According to rumors, a special invitation was sent to all the kings and demons of the underworld, and a human sacrifice may (or may not) have been involved.

It is said that Abe no Seimei used the Lord Taizan Ceremony on his own deceased father; the spell was also used routinely on emperors to keep them alive for a long time, ensuring their lengthy reigns.

The legendary diviner, dubbed the "Merlin of Japan," has an interesting origin story, of course. Once upon a time, a just man named Abe no Yasuna was visiting a shrine near the Shinoda Forest when he saw a group of hunters chasing a white fox. Feeling pity for the poor animal, Abe no Yasuna chased after them and managed to save the fox, but not before getting hurt himself.

As he lay injured and bleeding on the ground, a woman suddenly appeared, introduced herself as Kuzu no Ha, and helped him back home. In the following days, this mysterious woman continued to visit to help nurse him back to health. The two fell in love, got married, and had a son they named Dōjimaru.

Life was great until Dōjimaru turned five; at that age, he accidentally discovered that his mother, Kuzu no Ha, was, in fact, a white fox. Having been discovered, Kuzu no Ha lamented that she could no longer remain living among humans. Because she was under the command of the fox god, Inari Daimyōjin (AKA: Inari Ōkami in the Kitsune entry; 稲荷大明神), she had to leave.

Not long after she fled, a heartbroken and distraught Dōjimaru found a hastily written poem his mother had pinned to the door. It read: "If you miss me, come visit. Your grieving Kuzu no Ha in the Shinoda Forest."

Hoping to convince her to come back home, Dōjimaru and his father hiked deep into the woods, where they were greeted by a white fox. They watched as the animal transformed into Kuzu no Ha right before their eyes. She couldn't return home with them, she said, but she did present her son with a crystal ball and a golden box, saying the fox god, Inari Daimyōjin, wanted her to entrust the two treasures to him.

Later, Dōjimaru changed his name to Abe no Seimei and became the most powerful sorcerer to have ever worked in the imperial court, and the rest is history—or legend, as the case may be.

In Modern Stories

Abe no Seimei, various onmyōji, and the practice of Onmyōdō itself are extremely popular in books, manga, games, anime, TV shows, and movies. It's interesting to note, though, that in all the original images of Abe no Seimei, he is presented as an older, somewhat plump man, wearing fancy

Heian-style robes. But in recent years, you'll instead find him depicted as an attractive young lad, tall and thin, with long, silky flowing hair, who practices his onmyōji with great flair.

NOW YOU KNOW

Abe no Seimei's special symbol is the pentagram, which represents the Five Elements. You can buy ofuda (お札), a kind of good-luck charm, at the Seimei Jinja Shrine dedicated to him in Kyoto.

AKANAME

垢嘗

Pronunciation: AH-kah-NAH-may

Translation: The Filth Licker or Scum Licker

Etymology: The first character *aka* doesn't mean "red," like some people think when they first see the word—instead, it means "dirt," "grime," "filth," or "old skin that comes off while exfoliating." The second character means "to lick or taste something."

Similar to: Akaneburi (垢舐)

Overview

The akaname is a grotesque-looking yōkai that appears in the middle of the night to lick the accumulated dirt and scum from your bathtub—the dirtier, the better. The very first depiction of the akaname can be found in Toriyama Sekien's collection *Gazu Hyakki Yagyō* (画図百鬼夜行), which is translated as *Illustrated Demon Horde's Night Parade*. Published in 1776, this was Sekien's first book illustrating all manner of strange phenomena and yōkai beasties; it was such a hit that it spurred him to write three sequels.

In his book, Sekien did not provide much details about this particular muck-loving beastie, other than a black-and-white visual and a name. From the image, you can see an old-fashioned bathhouse with a skinny, most-likely-naked creature stepping from around a corner. It has a shock of black hair, a long tongue lolling out, and a single foot with one large clawed toe.

Later, the yōkai was elaborated on—in stories and art—and that's when we learned that the akaname's main purpose in life is to creep around bathhouses at night and lick the scum, mold, and residue from the tubs, floors, and walls. The akaname is a child-sized creature; it crouches or crawls across the floor, hunched over, on its clawed hands and feet. It has large goggling eyes; wild, mussed-up hair; and, most importantly, an incredibly long tongue. An akaname's skin color can range from blue-black to green to pale and is even sometimes depicted in a ruddy color when artists play off the homophone of *aka*, 赤, which can mean "red."

Despite its horrific appearance, this yōkai is benign. The akaname isn't really out to hurt you—it just wants to feed off your scum, late at night, in the dark, when you're not looking. If you do happen to come across one, it's anyone's guess which one of you will be more startled and run away first.

Background and Popular Stories

Before the akaname, there was the akaneburi (垢舐), which can be traced back to the year 1686. Yamaoka Genrin talked about this creature in his book of yōkai and ghost stories, *Kokon Hyaku Monogatari Hyōban* (古今百物語評判), or *A Critique of a Hundred Tales Old and New*. He wrote that an akaneburi is a monster created from the ki (気), or energy, of accumulated dirt and dust in old bathhouses and abandoned buildings. It then continues to live there, surviving by consuming the grime that spawned it. Genrin explained that just as fish are born in water and drink water, the akaneburi is a creature that originates from the buildup of scum and then eats scum to live.

There's an atypical and more sinister account of this detritivore (animal that eats dead organic material) written in *Nittō Honzō Zusan* (日東本草図纂), or *An Illustrated Compilation of Japanese Medicinal Herbs from the Eastern Regions*. A retelling of the horror-story version goes something like this: Once upon a time, there was a man who lived in Harima Province (what is now the southwestern part of Hyōgo Prefecture). His favorite pastime was to enjoy a nice long soak in an out-of-the-way outdoor hot spring called an onsen. There, he could get away from the hustle and bustle of the town and be alone. This fellow had been frequenting the onsen for quite some time and had never been disturbed by a single person—that is, until one day when, out of nowhere, a beautiful woman appeared. The man was understandably surprised, but was even more surprised when she offered to scrub his back for him. It seemed like a good idea at the time, so he agreed and turned his back to the stranger.

This turned out to be a deadly mistake. The beautiful woman was not a woman at all, but an akaneburi in disguise. With the man's back turned, the akaneburi stuck out its long, fearsome tongue and licked away his skin and flesh until he was nothing but a pile of bones.

In Modern Stories

The akaname shows up in the anime *GeGeGe no Kitarō* as a lanky, green-skinned, long-haired beastie and in the role-playing game Pathfinder as a ghoulish little troll. You can even find a detailed, blobby, foul-tempered minia-ture interpretation of the monster (complete with lengthy tongue) in the Mal-ifaux: Akaname collection of Wyrd Games. In the Japanese media franchise *Yo-kai Watch*, it's been given a much more adorable appearance and carries around its own dirty washbasin to lick. The English translation of this akaname is "Tublappa." Finally, let's not forget the most adorable pink versions of this gross little yōkai, the Pokémon Lickitung and Lickilicky.

AMABIE
アマビエ

Pronunciation: AH-mah-BEE-ay

Also known as: Amabiko (尼彦, 雨彦, 天彦),
sometimes pronounced Amahiko

Overview

The amabie is a glowing scaled sea creature with a beak and long hair. The yōkai suddenly appeared off the coast of Japan in the mid-1800s and warned of a widespread illness. It then urged the man who first encountered it to draw its likeness and show it to others, and instructed that he should encourage those who looked upon the drawing to do the same. The amabie promised that everyone who did so would be protected from disease and spared misfortune.

This clairvoyant ocean dweller was all but forgotten until COVID-19, when its extremely rough and utterly charming image returned along with a message of hope. Mizuki Productions (the production company of the late Mizuki Shigeru, the creator of the *GeGeGe no Kitarō* manga and anime) revived this magical mermaid-like creature in a single tweet. On March 17, 2020, they shared Mizuki Shigeru's own drawing of the yōkai, explained the story of the amabie, and wished for the current pandemic to disappear.

Almost immediately after the Mizuki Productions' social media post, the #amabiechallenge began, and people all across Japan—and, not long after, all

throughout the world—began sharing their own paintings, sketches, animations, crocheted dolls, embroidery, clay sculptures, food creations, and sweets of the yōkai. There was no end to the creativity and fun people were having, as they all came together with the same wish: for the pandemic to end soon.

Japan's health ministry quickly made the amabie the face of their public campaign, and the little design was everywhere: on signs, masks, cookies, amulets, keychains, and many more items.

Background and Popular Stories

The most commonly recounted story of the amabie reportedly happened in mid-May 1846 in what is now Kumamoto Prefecture. At that time, a shining object kept surfacing at night offshore. A town official was told to go and investigate; when he did, he was alarmed to find the bewildering creature waiting for him on the beach. This luminous sea monster, with its long hair, thick beak, and scales running from its neck to the bottom of its three legs (or fins), introduced itself, saying, "I am an amabie and I live in the ocean. Good harvests will continue for six years, but soon plagues will spread. Please draw me and show that drawing to others." The insinuation was that those who drew its likeness and motivated others to do the same would avoid the epidemic. The amabie then returned to the sea.

The town official did exactly as he was directed and reported the whole meeting and conversation, complete with a woodblock print of what the radiant sea monster looked like. This was published via kawaraban (瓦版), a single-sheet woodblock print that was used before newspapers to recount news, festivals, important current events, disasters, and even gossip. The town official's depiction is usually used as the basis for the images you see today.

There is another version of the amabie, called an amabiko, that is more apelike and completely covered in hair. While it may not be as dazzling, it is rather adorable, with its bulbous nose and funny body shape.

The amabie and amabiko aren't the only yōkai with portending abilities. They are just two of the several yogenjū (予言獣), or prophetic beasts. From the Edo era (1603–1867) to the Meiji era (1868–1912), epidemics like cholera, measles, smallpox, and the flu plagued Japan, killing many and, on occasion, decimating the population. During these times, there was a rise in the appearances of yogenjū.

Aside from the amabie, there were two other mermaid-type yogenjū who foretold the state of future crops as well as impending rampant disease. The first one was called the jinja-hime (神社姫), which literally means "shrine princess" (see the Ningyo entry for a story about her). She was a 20-foot-long (6-meter) serpentine beastie with the face of a woman, two horns, and a vermillion-colored belly. She announced that she was a messenger of Ryūjin (龍神), the dragon god who lives under the sea in his dragon palace, called Ryūgū-jō (see the Ryū entry for more about dragons).

The second was the hime-uo (姫魚), which literally translates to "princess fish." She first appeared in 1819 in Hirado, Hizen Province (now Nagasaki Prefecture) a couple of years before the first case of cholera broke out. She also looked like a mermaid, with black hair, horns, and a woman's face—but she was all fish from the neck down. Similarly, she predicted good harvests for seven years and the cholera epidemic. She advised people to draw and share her likeness, then she vanished under the waves. She was also a messenger from Ryūgū-jō, the dragon palace.

If the jinja-hime and hime-uo sound a lot alike to you, you're correct. You can tell the difference, though, because the jinja-hime is longer and more snakelike, with a bright red underbelly, whereas the hime-uo is shorter and has a golden body that resembles a fish.

Then—not fishlike at all and unrelated to the sea—there are the kudan and kutabe. Often believed to be born from cows, these two make their divine forecasts speaking human language and then die soon after. The kudan (件) has the face of a human and the body of a cow. It showed up in 1836 in Kyoto forecasting something similar to what the other prophetic beasts foretold: There would be some great harvests but also a terrible disease. But it said that if people hung up its image, their families would be safe, and their fields would be bountiful. There have been quite a few sightings of the kudan, where it foresees everything from crop failures to droughts to war and, of course, sickness.

A second human-faced bovine, and a variant of the kudan, is the kutabe (クタベ). It turned up toward the end of the Edo era in Tateyama, Toyama Prefecture, stating that a difficult disease of unknown cause would spread, but those who saw the kutabe would be saved. Some say *kutabe* is just *kudan* pronounced in a different dialect. But unlike the kudan, the kutabe never predicted bumper crops.

Both the kudan and the kutabe most likely derived from a Chinese mythical creature called the bai ze, or hakutaku (白沢) in Japanese. This is yet another human-faced, beast-bodied yōkai. This one, though, has three eyes on its head, three on each side of its body, and six horns. It was considered extremely lucky, and its image in charms and talismans was also distributed during the Edo era (see the Baku entry for another mythical beast based off the hakutaku).

In Modern Stories

The amabie can be seen in *GeGeGe no Kitarō*, both the manga and the anime, as well as *Yo-kai Watch* and the trading card game Yu-Gi-Oh!, where it's super kawaii and colorful, with long blue hair and starry anime eyes.

NOW YOU KNOW

It's worth mentioning that the name *amabie* is most likely a copying mistake. There is only one recorded mention of an *amabie* and many more using the name *amabiko* or *amahiko*. Therefore, it isn't out of the question to think the person who carved the *amabie* version mistook the last character *e* (エ) for the similar-looking character *ko* (コ).

AZUKIARAI

小豆洗い

Pronunciation: AH-zoo-key-AH-rye

Translation: The Red Bean Washer

Etymology: The first two characters (小豆) mean
"small" and "bean," referring to azuki beans.
The second word (洗い) means "to wash."

Also known as: Azukitogi (小豆研ぎ), Azukiage (小豆アゲ),
and Azuki Goshagosha (小豆ごしゃごしゃ)

Similar to: Azukihakari (小豆はかり), Azukibāba (あずき婆), Kuneyusuri
(くねゆすり), Sentaku Kitsune (洗濯狐)
and Kometogi Bāba (米とぎ婆)

Overview

The azukiarai is a mysterious yōkai that is almost always heard and not seen. Nevertheless, it's not difficult to find a description or image of this creepy little fellow. As far back as 1841, in volume 5 of *Ehon Hyaku Monogatari* (絵本百物語), or the *Picture Book of a Hundred Stories*, Takehara Shunsensai gives us a colored illustration of this unnerving diminutive man-creature. In it, he's standing by a riverbank with his bald head, clawed feet, large eyes, and toothy grin. He's hunched over a wooden bowl, reaching in, presumably concentrating on doing what he's always doing: bean washing.

It's said if you're hiking through the mountains and suddenly catch a sound like *shoki-shoki, shoki-shoki,* it *could* be the sound of water trickling over river stones and echoing through the valley—or, it could be the azukiarai, out there in the middle of nowhere, humming a little tune as he works. There's no need to be afraid, though. This old-man-looking yōkai is harmless—at least that's what everyone says. But that song he sings does have some unsettling lyrics:

"Shoki-shoki! Shall I wash the beans?
Or shall I catch and eat a human being?
Shoki-shoki!"

This unnerving ditty might explain why so few people have ever actually laid eyes on an azukiarai. If you were out in the middle of nowhere and heard that song, you probably wouldn't stick around to find out who was singing it either.

Throughout Japan, there are differing theories about what the azukiarai really is. Some people believe the sound is caused by a weasel crying out or wagging its tail. In other places, it is attributed to a variety of animals, such as the tanuki (Japanese raccoon dogs), foxes, otters, or even giant toads called gama-gaeru, either shaking their bodies or rubbing the warts on their backs against one another.

Background and Popular Stories

Usually, azukiarai are found outdoors near rivers, but there is one variety that resides in houses and temples. These bean washers may be male or female, and they tend to be active in the middle of the night while folks are trying to sleep. If you've woken up after hearing a disturbance and expect to find the enigmatic bean washer in your home, you'd most likely find nothing at all, since the azukiarai are rumored to be heard, not seen.

There might be an explanation for this. Long before neatly sealed houses and bug spray, people lived closer to insects, or insects preferred to live closer to people, nestling in their homes. One of these bugs was nicknamed the chatate mushi (茶たて虫), which means "tea-making insect." As the vermin munched on paper or mold or rubbed its wings together, the noise would reverberate off the taut shoji windows, creating a sound similar to someone whisking—or making—green tea. In a quiet house at night, this same sound could be mistaken for someone stirring beans in a colander. Because of this, the insect earned a second nickname: the "azukiarai mushi" or "azukiarai bug."

There is another tale in a book written in the Edo era (1603–1867) called *Kaidan Oi no Tsue* (怪談老の杖). It tells the story of a temple; when night fell, the sound of someone tossing dried azuki beans onto the attic floor could be heard from within. The noise would grow louder and louder until it seemed as if 5 gallons (18 liters) of azuki beans were being scattered across the floor. This was dubbed the "ceiling azukiarai" or the "azukihakari."

There are different origin stories, but the following tale found in *Ehon Hyaku Monogatari*, simply titled *Azukiarai*, seems to be the best known. According to the story, at a temple in Takada, Echigo Province (present-day Joetsu City, Niigata Prefecture), there was a young monk named Nichigen (日顕). Nichigen had a physical disability, and he also had a talent for counting things and guessing measurements with amazing accuracy. He could look at a pile of azuki beans and tell exactly if it equaled one gō or one shō (these are old measurements—a gō is 6.1 ounces, or 180.4 milliliters, and is one-tenth of a shō, which is 61 ounces, or 1.804 liters).

The head abbot of the temple favored Nichigen and was even planning on making him his successor. That news didn't settle very well with another monk named Enkai (円海), who was evil-hearted and envious of the young Nichigen. One day, Enkai seized Nichigen and threw him down a well, killing him.

Thereafter, the spirit of the poor dead monk would throw azuki beans against the temple's wooden rain shutters from dusk until nightfall, then go down by the river and wash and count beans. The murderous Enkai was sentenced to death. Today, if you are able to find the well where Nichigen died, it is said you can hear him and Enkai arguing.

In Modern Stories

The azukiarai is a recurring character in the manga and anime *GeGeGe no Kitarō* and also appears in the 2005 movie *The Great Yokai War,* directed by Takashi Miike.

NOW YOU KNOW

Another version of the azukiarai story from the Hinohara area of Tokyo describes a woman who was scolded by her mother-in-law after she found pebbles mixed in with the beans. The woman was so distraught and ashamed that she threw herself into the river and died. The sound of someone washing beans could be heard from the area after that.

BAKENEKO
AND NEKOMATA
化け猫 and 猫股 or 猫又

Pronunciations: BAH-keh-NEH-koh and NEH-koh-MAH-tah

Translation: Bakeneko: Changed Cat, Monster Cat,
Goblin Cat; Nekomata: Fork-Tailed Cat

Similar to: Kaibyō (怪猫), which literally means "strange cat."
All supernatural cats fall under the category of kaibyō: bakeneko,
nekomata, and maneki neko (beckoning cat)

Overview

Both the bakeneko and the nekomata are cat yōkai known for their shape-shifting abilities and propensity to cause mischief and mayhem. Nekomata are typically recognized by their distinctive two tails, while bakeneko either appear as a normal cat or as an enormous one, sometimes with an inordinately long tail. They've probably been around since the feline's first arrival in Japan, a date that isn't exactly known. However, there are writings and artwork dating as far back as the early Heian era (C.E. 794–1185) that depict these frisky critters entertaining emperors and defending the delicious calligraphy-on-vellum Buddhist sutras from rats.

Having said that, Japan has always had a complicated relationship with cats. On one hand, what's not to love about a cat? On the other hand, there's always the chance your beloved pet will suffer "the change" and become something weird, mischievous, or just downright deadly.

Background and Popular Stories

The more you read about the bakeneko and the nekomata, the more confused you might become. Since both of these creatures have inhabited all parts of Japan for so long, their stories have become intermingled, separately elaborated upon, and simply, well, changed.

There is an old diary entry that seems to be the first instance of a nekomata documented in writing. It dates back to 1233 and was written by Fujiwara no Teika. This lover of journals meticulously kept one throughout his life. In one of his entries, he wrote that a beastly creature came from Nara. It had catlike eyes and a doglike body. It also killed and ate seven (or eight) people in a single night. The diarist didn't exactly specify that this was a yōkai, per se, but he did give it a name: *nekomata.*

Regional differences aside, here's what we know: Both the bakeneko and the nekomata start out as a regular, run-of-the-mill, non-supernatural cat, usually one that has lived to reach an impressive, venerable old age. The change from normal cat to yōkai can happen at any age from as early as seven years to as late as twenty. You never know, though, and that's part of the mystery and the gamble of owning a cat in Japan.

There are incidences, however, especially in the case of the bakeneko, where the change happens after a cat has died tragically at the hands of a human and then comes back to get its revenge. In those cases, it's more of a ghost cat.

The bakeneko and the nekomata are different yōkai, but there's a lot of overlap in what they do and how to tell them apart. As it turns out, there are two varieties of nekomata: the ordinary elderly house cat and the mountain cat.

The first is small and—for a lack of a better word—catlike (except for its forked tail), while the second can grow up to 10 feet (3 meters) in length and hunts bears, wild boars, and people. This latter mountain-variety nekomata may or may not have the forked tail. The bakeneko, however, looks like anything from a normal cat to an enormous angry monster cat—it can even look like your neighbor! It's believed they can shape-shift into people when the urge strikes.

In general, the nekomata is the more dangerous of the two. But they can both be silly mischief makers too; they'll walk upright, don tenugui cloths on their heads, and dance around people's pillows on their hind legs while they try to sleep.

Some can talk as well. There's an account from 1683 of someone spotting a cat at a temple, chatting up a bunch of neighborhood strays. Then a little later, a nekomata was seen on a nearby roof. Suddenly, losing its footing, it slipped and fell, invoking the name of the Buddha as it did.

Some bakeneko and nekomata can transform into human form; some choose to possess people, while others prefer to hide in the shadows, waiting to pounce and attack random passersby. Everyone, though, can probably agree that the most disturbing proclivity of the nekomata is when it engages in necromancy.

Yes, these beastly felines have been known to not only raise the dead but manipulate them as well. There's one old story of a cat sneaking into a room where a newly deceased body lay in repose. Moments later, the corpse hopped up and started wildly dancing around. When others were called to help, the dear departed climbed out a window and onto the roof. There it scampered about before jumping off and disappearing. The body was found in a field a few days later—dead for real, this time.

Many books on folklore and culture in Japan detail these types of fascinating incidences as reason for the country's love-fear relationship with the cat. People loved cats but were afraid of them eventually turning into murderous, dead-raising monsters. So, sometimes when a family got a cat as a pet, they would decide right away how long they wanted to keep the animal. Knowing that it would be risky to keep it for longer than seven years, they would sit the kitten down and address it directly, saying, for example, "This is your home for five years. You are a five-year cat." The stories go that when the time limit was up, the cat would, hopefully, of its own volition, wander off into the mountains, leaving the family safer but no doubt lonelier. It's not written if anyone considered that this practice might add to the number of mountain nekomata that relentlessly terrorized travelers and wild animals.

The following is a list of questions you can use to determine whether or not your cat has changed into a yōkai. If you can answer yes to any or all of these, you might just have a nekomata on your hands.

1. When it's dark and you pet your cat the wrong way, against the line of the fur, does the skin glow?
2. Have you caught your cat licking the oil from your oil lamps?
3. Has your cat's tail gotten longer? Does it move like a snake so much so that it gives you the willies?
4. Does your cat prefer to be around smelly things, especially cuddling up next to dead people?
5. Does your cat have two tails?
6. When no one is around, does your cat start a fire in the hearth or enjoy starting fires in general?

In Modern Stories

The bakeneko and the nekomata have proven again and again their tenacity and long lives in pop culture. Today you can find them in all sorts of anime and manga, like *Naruto* and *Inuyasha* (Kirara), and in *GeGeGe no Kitarō* as one of the main characters, Nekomusume. Let's not forget the clowder of yōkai-based cats in Pokémon either—Purrloin, Espurr, Meowstic, and Espeon.

BAKU
獏

Pronunciation: BAH-koo

Translation: The Dream Eater

Similar to: Hakutaku (白沢)

Overview

The baku, or dream eater, is probably one of the more beloved beasts in the yōkai pantheon. This little critter resembles the nue (see Nue entry later in this book) in that it is composed of parts borrowed from various animals. Popular depictions describe it as having a longish nose like an elephant, four striped feet like a tiger, the body of a bear, and the eyes and ears of a rhino. It sports two small tusks and flicks the tail of an ox.

In other writings and works of art, you'll find the baku put together piecemeal, with animal parts used in different combinations. So, keep in mind, contrasting interpretations of this fanciful beast abound, depending on the artwork or story passed down. Regardless, having a varying fantastical form is totally on brand for a nighttime creature that works with dreams.

One explanation as to why it is such a patchwork beast is that when the gods were done creating all the animals, they looked around, gathered up the scraps of what was left, and cobbled together the baku.

Background and Popular Stories

Like many of Japan's mythical creatures, the baku originally came from China, arriving sometime between the sixth century (along with Buddhism) and the fifteenth century (accounts vary). The Chinese version of the baku had an entirely different duty; its job was to offer protection to a person from pestilence and evil. Once in Japan, this chimera shifted into more of a nightmare eater. In fact, it needs nightmares to survive.

It's said that back in the day, children who woke from nightmares would know to repeat three times, "Baku-san, come eat my dream." There are several different versions of this chant, one being, "Kono yume, baku ni agemasu," which literally means, "I give this dream to the baku."

However you phrased it, after repeating the prayer three times, the baku would enter your room, slink its way over, and gobble up your distressing dream. You would then never have that particular nightmare again. The bizarre-looking baku spent long nights hopping from rooftop to rooftop, listening for someone to call out so it could hurry over and feast.

Back in the Muromachi era (1336–1573), a person who was on their deathbed would be given an image of the baku to hold as protection against evil spirits. More recently, in the Edo era (1603–1867), baku "pillows" were employed to fend off nightmares. These pillows were not the kind we have today—in that time, they consisted of a small cloth tube filled with rice, soba, or buckwheat husks that was tied to a wood or ceramic block. It was the bottom, hard part of the pillow that could be shaped like a baku or have one painted on or carved into it. Later, after modern pillows arrived, talismans or drawings were slipped under them, or even embroidered on pillowcases, all to ensure pleasant dreams.

If you ever find yourself visiting a temple or shrine in Japan, look up at the corners of those fancy curved roofs. There you can sometimes find gorgeously ornate and colorful carvings of this lucky divine creature. It's easily identifiable by its long nose and tusks.

It's worth pointing out that the word *baku* can also refer to an actual animal, the Asian tapir, which physically resembles some of the descriptions of these legendary dream eaters. Like the baku, the tapir has a trunk-like nose, interesting body shape, and markings (especially the young ones). Even the kanji characters for *baku* and *tapir* are the same.

The prolific author Lafcadio Hearn wrote a delightful old folktale told in the first person about the baku, which demonstrates the creature's character quite well. His story goes like this:

Once upon a time, during one of the hottest days of the year, I wakened, miserable from the heat, just in time to see a baku come in through my window.

"Have you anything for me to eat?" it asked.

I was happy and relieved to hear this request, for I'd just had the strangest of dreams.

"Assuredly!" I said. "Listen to my dream!"

I then went on to describe my dream of being in a room, looking at my own dead body. There were people dressed in black sitting around it. The lamps burned as the atmosphere in the room thickened, and I could feel the people were afraid. One by one, they left the room, until I was there alone with my corpse.

I went over to more closely observe it, stooping and looking at my face, when suddenly the eyes opened! My other self sprang at me and fastened itself to me, moaning and gnawing and rending.

I found an axe in my hand and struck it over and over until it lay there before me a shapeless, hideous, reeking mass, the abominable ruin of myself.

"Please, baku, eat this horrible dream!"

"Nay," said the creature. "I never eat lucky dreams. That was a lucky and fortunate dream. I believe in Buddhism, and in this dream, the axe represents the Excellent Law of Buddhism, and it has destroyed the monster of self, your ego. This is the best kind of dream!"

Then the baku left through the window. I looked after him and beheld him fleeing over the miles of moonlit roofs, passing from housetop to housetop, with amazing soundless leaps, like a great cat.

In Modern Stories

Of course, there are several Pokémon based on such a curiously adorable little beast—those would be Drowzee, Hypno, Munna, and Musharna. There is even a Pokémon technique, albeit rare, called Dream Eater. There's also a manga derived from this creature called *Nightmare Inspector*. Speaking of manga, author Neil Gaiman's graphic novel *Sandman: The Dream Hunters* (illustrated by Yoshitaka Amano) is a story about a monk, a fox spirit, a tanuki (Japanese raccoon dog), and a baku. The baku is also mentioned in the TV show *Supernatural*, but flipping the creature's powers. The show mentions that the baku will induce terrible nightmares instead of sweeping them away.

NOW YOU KNOW

There is one caution to keep in mind when dealing with a baku. If you call on it too often, it will get greedy and won't stop devouring your nightmares. It will proceed to consume your dreams, hopes, and aspirations, leaving you with an entirely meaningless life.

BINBŌGAMI

貧乏神

Pronunciation: BEEN-boh-GAH-mee

Translation: The God of Poverty

Etymology: *Binbō* means "poor" or "poverty." *Gami* is the same as *kami* and can mean "god," "spirit," or "deity;" this term encompasses both good and bad forces or spirits.

Overview

The binbōgami is a yōkai that brings impoverishment and ill fortune to everyone it encounters. If this poverty god decides to live in your house—not that you'll necessarily know, because it's wily and keeps hidden—it'll drive out all your good luck, leaving you poor and miserable.

An 1884 painting by Tsukioka Yoshitoshi entitled *Jakikyūki* (邪鬼窮鬼), which literally means "Harmful Demon, Poor Demon" but carries the English title *Demons of Illness and Poverty Stalking the Lucky Gods*, shows us an early depiction of what the binbōgami might look like. The painting shows a destitute-looking pair of creatures; the one that looks like a skinny, dirty old man wearing tattered clothes and waving a paper fan is the binbōgami.

Why is the binbōgami considered a "god"? That's because, remarkably, this wretched deity can also be found mentioned in Buddhist scriptures, specifically in the Daihatsu Nehankyō sutra (大般涅槃教), also known as the

Mahāparinirvana sutra. Even more surprising is that although almost all the depictions of the binbōgami today are of a filthy old man, in these sacred texts, it was said to be a woman. She's referred to politely as the "Venerable God of Poverty" and called Kokuanten (黒闇天, which is the kanji for "black darkness" combined with the character for "heaven").

Kokuanten invites bad luck and disaster, but she has a beautiful older sister named Kisshōten or Kichijōten (吉祥天) who is the goddess of auspicious fortune; she brings beauty, fertility, abundance, and happiness to all.

Background and Popular Stories

Have you ever known someone who just can't seem to hang on to money, or who is constantly plagued by one unfortunate event after another? Well, in Japan, someone might say that person either is a binbōgami, is living with one, or has one clinging on to them. There doesn't seem to be any rhyme or reason as to why this poverty god would attach itself to you or your house.

It is rumored, though, that the binbōgami loves the rich savory smell of grilling fermented bean paste, called yakimiso (焼き味噌). For this reason, it's suggested you should never broil miso at home, lest you inadvertently call this unfavorable god.

Speaking of the savory aroma of charbroiled miso, the binbōgami is almost always seen holding a frayed paper fan called a shibu uchiwa (渋団扇). This is a traditional fan that is coated with persimmon tannin to make the delicate washi paper stronger, longer lasting, and insect repellent. The poverty god uses this ever-present tool not to cool itself off, but to waft the delicious smell of grilling miso its way. But be careful, because the shibu uchiwa also has the power to make people more and more poor.

Since no one knows how to avoid the binbōgami (other than not broiling miso), the trick is to know how to get rid of it. In Japan, there's a shrine for nearly everything, so of course, there is one dedicated to the binbōgami or, more precisely, expelling it from your life. One such shrine is called Binbōgami

Jinja, located in Iida City, Nagano Prefecture, and it is having a lot of fun with this yōkai. This binbōgami shrine is situated in the very back of a store and warehouse that makes and sells miso. Inside, you'll find a giant miso barrel cut open to reveal an extremely gloomy-looking wooden statue of the yōkai, a large tree stump (the "Sacred Tree"), a stick that has been named "bin bō" (which is a pun off the words for stick, bō, and poverty), and instructions.

Usually, when greeting or addressing one of Japan's many deities, you place your hands together and pray. Here, the directions state, whatever you do, *don't* do that. Instead, use the binbō stick to hit the tree trunk three times as hard as you like, proclaiming, "Binbōgami deteke!" or "Binbōgami, go away!"

Next, kick the tree trunk three times, repeating the same phrase, and then, finally, take a handful of beans from a box provided and throw them into the barrel at the effigy of the unlucky deity, stating that you wish to expel the poverty god that is living in your heart. There is also a list of positive statements you can recite in order to shift your luck. The trick for ridding yourself of a binbōgami might not be banishing it, but changing your way of thinking.

One popular story about the binbōgami seems to back up that theory. Once, the beautiful and refined good-luck goddess, Kisshōten, visited a random house. The owner of the house, realizing who she was, excitedly invited her in and made sure she was comfortable, treating her like the goddess she was.

After some time, there was another visitor at the door: the ominous and unlucky goddess Kokuanten. The owner of the house, seeing this shabbily dressed and dirty deity, was furious and chased her away. Relieved that he was able to get rid of her, he returned to his elegant guest, but found her already walking to the door. As she left, she said to him, "That was my sister, Kokuanten. We go everywhere together. We're two halves of a whole, and without her, there is no me."

And she left.

This story teaches that both the god(dess) of poverty and the god(dess) of fortune are two sides of the same coin.

In Modern Stories

There's a Japanese manga and thirteen-episode anime written and illustrated by Yoshiaki Sukeno; it's called *Binbōgami ga!* (*The Binbōgami!*) and has been translated into English as *Good Luck Girl!* The story revolves around a spoiled high school girl who has always had exceptional luck, often drawing it from her surroundings. In order to rebalance the world, the god of misfortune is sent to the human world (in the guise of another teenage girl) to steal some of her luck.

NOW YOU KNOW

Remember the poverty god's special fan? Well, there's an idiom, "binbōgami no shibu uchiwa (貧乏神の渋団扇)," or "the frugal fan of the binbōgami." It's a metaphor for something that exacerbates poverty. For example, this could refer to someone who spends all their savings on lottery tickets, hoping to win—when, in fact, they end up losing more money and are now even worse off than when they started. That situation would be just like "the frugal fan of the binbōgami."

DOROTABŌ
泥田坊

Pronunciation: DOH-roh-TAH-boh

Translation: Mud-Field Goblin, Muddy-Field Monk

Overview

The dorotabō is a filth-caked, one-eyed, bald-headed yōkai that emerges from a muddy rice field in the middle of the night, raising its two three-fingered hands in the air as it howls in resentment and anger: "Ta wo kaese!" or "Return my rice fields!"

This muddy-field goblin is a sad, messy monster that is justified in its rage. Before becoming the dorotabō, the creature was a regular man; while he was alive in human form, he bought a rice field and tended it all throughout his adult life so he could provide for his family and bequeath it to his grandchildren. But after his death, it was sold to someone else by his ungrateful, lazy, sake-drinking adult children, and it now lies fallow. He has returned to haunt the fields as the dreaded dorotabō to demand the return of his land.

The dorotabō legends are peculiar. Other than Toriyama Sekien's depiction in *Konjaku Hyakki Shūi* (今昔百機種位), or *Supplement to the Hundred Demons from the Present and the Past* (1781), there are no other mentions of this mucky monster in early texts or art. The appearances that came after imitated Sekien's piece. It's well known that Sekien didn't just give likenesses to old folktales and myths; he made up his own creatures too. The dorotabō very well might be one of those Sekien-original yōkai, and a humorous one at that.

In his woodblock print, Sekien gives the dorotabō only three fingers on each hand. This is a trait often found in images of oni (ogres) and other wicked creatures. There are different theories as to why this association exists, but one is that in Buddhism, monks use their hands when reciting the five states of the human heart and mind. Two fingers represent humanity's virtues—wisdom, or chie (智慧), and compassion, or jihi (慈悲)—while the other three symbolize the poisons of humanity, described as ton-jin-chi (貪・瞋・痴): jealousy and greed, hatred and anger, and delusion and ignorance. Scholars and folklorists alike have hypothesized that dorotabō (as well as other beastly monsters) have only three digits on each hand because they possess only those three negative traits and lack the goodness of wisdom and compassion that humans have.

Background and Popular Stories

The yōkai researcher and author Katsumi Tada has a theory about the origins of the dorotabō. Considering that the first image of this filth-covered monster was made by Toriyama Sekien, who never said no to a good pun, Tada suggests the term *dorotabō* is actually wordplay.

He may be on to something. Consider, for example, the poet Dorotabō Yumenari (泥田坊夢成), who lived during Sekien's time. This particular poet wrote kyōka (狂歌), a type of poetry that was full of playful verses and vulgar turns of phrase. Dorotabō Yumenari often visited the Yoshiwara pleasure quarters, and would spend all his money on women and sake. It's possible Sekien was playfully castigating the poet for living a little too recklessly when crafting the yōkai dorotabō.

To give another example: When Sekien included his image of the dorotabō in his collection *Konjaku Hyakki Shūi*, a new red light district opened north of the capital Edo. It was called Hokkoku, or the Northern Country, but

nicknamed "Yoshiwara Tanbo," or "Yoshiwara Rice Fields"—"rice fields" being a nickname for brothels in Sekien's time. Perhaps Sekien was alluding to this red light district in his tale of the dorotabō.

To go even further: In the story, the dorotabō calls out, "Ta wo kaese!" meaning, "Return my rice fields!" This phrase sounds very similar to *ta wo tagaese* (耕せ), which means to "plow the fields." This could be another play on words, in which Sekien seems to be alluding to sexual intercourse. There is also the old Japanese idiom "doro ta wo bō de utsu"(泥田を棒で打つ), which literally means, "hitting a muddy field with a stick." This is another euphemism for the pleasures of the adult entertainment quarter, and Sekien probably could not help himself but to reference it while creating this muddy yōkai.

The typical tale of the dorotabō goes something like this: Once, long ago, there was a man who lived in the Hokkoku, or Northern Country. He wanted to leave his grandchildren something of value—something that would ensure they had plenty of food and a solid way to make a living. After some thought, he bought a piece of land and turned it into a rice field. For many years, he selflessly plowed the field, planted seedlings, and grew and harvested rice. No matter how bad the weather or how much his body ached, he continued to toil away and never complained.

Meanwhile, his own adult children stayed at home and did nothing at all. They watched him work, ate his rice, and spent his money, never once lifting a finger to help. The old man grew older, maintaining the farm until the day he died.

At first, his children lived off the money he had left them, though they quickly frittered it away on alcohol. When it disappeared, they sold the land and used that money to carry on their degenerate lives. The rice field was never properly cared for by the new owners either. It wasn't long after that, late one evening, that a dark-colored mud beast rose up out of the ground and began calling, "Give me back my rice fields!"

The spirit of the old man, full of bitterness and disgust at seeing what had become of his land and years of careful hard work, had returned. The very earth that the farmer had tended so diligently with unwavering devotion had transformed into the gruesome dorotabō. Every night, this muck-dripping, one-eyed apparition would emerge from the fields, its anguished cries shouting its displeasure, a relentless demand for the return of the stolen rice fields.

In Modern Stories

The dorotabō can be found in products from the Japanese media franchise *Yo-kai Watch*, going by the name Mudmunch in English, and in Pokémon as Grimer and Muk. You'll notice both little monsters have only three fingers, like the original dorotabō, and seem to be rising up out of a puddle of filth. Then there is also a character Kabane Kusaka who is nicknamed Dorotabō in the manga *Kemono Jihen*.

NOW YOU KNOW

There are more recent accounts of the dorotabō too. During World War II, the government appropriated a lot of land from farmers so that military bases could be built to house and train soldiers. Many of the farmers, having no say in the matter, ended up dying by suicide. Some lost all their land and died homeless. Stories have been passed down of their angry spirits returning as dorotabō to curse those who stole their land.

FUTAKUCHI ONNA
ふた口女

Pronunciation: FOO-tah Koo-chee OHN-nah

Translation: The Two-Mouthed Woman

Similar to: Kuchinashi Onna (口無し女), the No-Mouthed Woman;
and Kuwazu Nyōbo (食わず女房), the Wife Who Didn't Eat

Overview

Futakuchi onna is one of those deceptively harmless looking yōkai that, at first glance, appears to be a nice young lady, but it turns out she has a surprise up her sleeve—or, in this case, beneath her long silky hair.

The thing that makes futakuchi onna distinctly nonhuman is the second mouth hidden on the back of her head (or sometimes at the nape of her neck). Only when it's time to eat does her hair part and the large hideous orifice reveals itself.

If you think that scenario is unsettling, wait until those flowing locks—wild with hunger—take on a life of their own and begin whipping around like shiny black snakes, snatching up nearby food and feeding it to the gaping maw that devours faster than any person could possibly eat. While futakuchi onna consumes all edible provisions in the house, fortunately, her appetite is limited to food alone, sparing any acts of cannibalism.

It's important to note that there is a very similar yōkai that is often mistaken for futakuchi onna called kuchinashi onna (口無し女), "the no-mouthed woman," or kuwazu nyōbo (食わず女房), "the wife who didn't eat."

Background and Popular Stories

Futakuchi onna's origin story starts almost like a Grimm's Fairy Tale but ends less happily. According to the 1841 book *Ehon Hyaku Monogatari* (絵本百物語), or the *Picture Book of a Hundred Stories*, by Takehara Shunsensai, futakuchi onna acquired this extra mouth as a result of a curse from a deceased stepchild. The tale starts off in a familar way: A man, after losing his wife, remarried. However, the new wife favored her own children over the man's only daughter. Instead of leaving the poor stepchild in the woods or making her scrub floors, this evil stepmother actually starved the girl to death.

The resentment and restless soul of this ghost baby sought revenge by cursing the stepmother. There are two versions of this curse; in the first, the stepmother's future children were born with an extra mouth on the back of their heads and were given a ravenous appetite. In the second, it's said that the wicked stepmother herself became a futakuchi onna, and it happened in the most unusual way.

On the forty-ninth day after the child's death, an accident occurred. A man hired to split firewood swung his axe and unintentionally sliced the back of the stepmother's head. It was a bad injury, but she survived—only, the lesion never completely healed. Over time, the wound started to look like two lips, and the still-exposed bone resembled teeth. There was even a swollen bit of flesh that appeared to be a tongue.

The stepmother experienced constant agonizing pain. Somehow, though, she discovered that if she placed some food in this "mouth" on the back of her head, this suffering would ease (see the Jinmensō entry for another parasitic yōkai that insists on being fed in order to alleviate its host's torment).

It wasn't long before the stepmother was eating with both mouths, and all the food in the house was disappearing at an alarming rate.

For those who thought this story couldn't get any creepier, occasionally, this new mouth murmured, "Apologize. Apologize."

The similar yōkai kuwazu nyōbo's tale is quite different. You'll find her even less discerning about what she eats. In her story, there was a rice farmer who decided he wanted to get married. He was very picky, though, and wrote up a list of requirements for a bride. She had to be beautiful and hardworking and have little to no appetite. The farmer toiled long in his fields and didn't want to share his rice with anyone, not even with his future wife.

Unsurprisingly, no such woman could be found, and it looked like he'd never find his perfect partner—that is, until one night while he was sitting outside in his wooden barrel tub. He was startled when the most beautiful woman he'd ever seen suddenly appeared out of the darkness. She introduced herself as new to the area and in need of employment and a place to stay. This stranger also mentioned that she wasn't afraid of hard work, and—the best part—she never ate.

The joyous farmer seized his good fortune. It wasn't long before the two were married and it was as if all his dreams had come true. He continued to work his fields while his new bride dragged the bags of harvested rice into the storehouse and took care of the home. True to her word, he never saw her eat a single bite of food.

Months went by and spring arrived. Readying to plant new seedlings, the farmer realized he hadn't admired all the rice stores recently. He pulled open the heavy door to the storehouse and, horror stricken, found the room almost empty. He questioned his wife, but she feigned ignorance. This raised his suspicions.

The next day, the farmer pretended to go out and till the fields but instead returned home and snuck up into the rafters. There he observed his delicate wife haul in the last of the previous year's harvest, cook it all in a large iron pot, and proceed to make a mountain of rice balls.

What came next was worse. The gentle beauty parted the back of her hair to expose an oversized second mouth, its drooling tongue greedily licking its lips. The long tresses then proceeded to grab the rice balls and drop them into the cavernous, gnashing hole one by one until they were all gone.

The horrified farmer realized that his perfect, noneating wife was in fact some kind of mountain witch. Later that evening, he made up a story about how she should return to her childhood home to take care of her aging parents. His wife obediently agreed to leave, but asked if she could take a long length of rope and the wooden barrel tub with her, and requested that he check the small leak in the tub before she left.

The farmer happily handed her the rope and climbed in to examine this hole she'd mentioned. Suddenly, she threw the rope around the tub, hoisted it onto her back, and bolted away. The farmer had been tricked. When he looked again, he saw his once-beautiful wife had transformed into a hideous yamauba ogress (a mountain witch). The oni wife—running far too fast for the farmer to leap out of the tub—cackled and told him she was taking him into the mountains to feed him to her hungry children.

The farmer almost gave up, but after some time, she stopped under a tree to rest. He quietly grabbed on to a branch and lifted himself out of the tub. Knowing she could easily track him down and outrun him, he found a patch of irises and hid inside them. Here he was safe because oni abhor iris flowers and their sharp, swordlike leaves.

In Modern Stories

Probably the best-known adaptation of this double-mouthed creature is the Pokémon Mawile. This Pocket Monster seems to have a large ponytail on the back of its head, but it also acts as a giant mouth. Then there is Mega Mawile, which has two such mouths, surely making futakuchi onna proud.

NOW YOU KNOW

In ancient times, the iris plant was used to ward off evil spirits in a spring ceremony called Tango no Sekku (端午の節句). The strong fragrance of the iris was also thought to purify the air and remove negative energy. Bathing with a handful of the leaves is an old tradition called shōbuyu (菖蒲湯), or "iris bath." It is believed to promote blood circulation, help with relaxation, as well as drive away harmful spirits and prevent contagious diseases, and it is enjoyed even today.

HASHIHIME

橋姫

Pronunciation: HAH-she-HEE-may

Translation: The Bridge Maiden or Bridge Princess

Also known as: Uji no Hashihime (宇治の橋姫),
the Bridge Princess of Uji

Overview

Hashihime is one of the oldest, most tragic, most terrifying, and most heart-breaking yōkai in the pantheon. She was a woman whose husband cheated on her, and in order to get revenge on him, she herself became an evil ogre.

Hashihime wasn't originally a yōkai. She was a normal person who lived over a thousand years ago. There isn't even a record of her real name, although she did become known as the Bridge Princess of Uji, even though it's very unlikely she was an actual princess.

Hashihime was mentioned as far back as C.E. 905 in the *Kokin Wakashū* (古今和歌集), or *Collection of Japanese Poems of Ancient and Modern Times*. She was referred to again in the eleventh-century work *The Tale of Genji*, where her name was actually the title of one of the chapters. She also appeared in the famous Noh play *Kanawa* (金輪), or *The Iron Crown* (or *Trivet*).

Background and Popular Stories

There is a reason Hashihime's dreadful tale has been told and retold over and over again—it's a good story. There are many variations of the legend, but at its core, it's a tale of betrayal, jealousy, and revenge. The following is a version based on the Noh play previously mentioned.

Once upon a time, a young woman fell in love and married a man who she trusted and adored. They moved away from her family and friends to the city of Kyoto. For a time, everything was wonderful, but quite often, her husband's new job kept him away. Still, she trusted him—that is, until she discovered he had a mistress.

Consumed by jealousy and rage, the woman walked for hours every night across the city and up the steep slopes of Mount Kurama to visit the Kifune Shrine (貴船神社), where an extremely powerful water dragon goddess named Takaokami (高龗神) was enshrined. The woman prayed until well after midnight, imploring the deity to help because she was weak and wished to become strong like an oni (ogre) and get her revenge.

On the seventh night, right before she arrived at the shrine, a priest there had a disturbing dream. In it, the goddess Takaokami ordered him to tell the young woman who was soon to arrive that she no longer needed to come to the shrine. Instead, she should return home and rub vermillion paste all over her face, neck, and body. Once her skin was dyed the deep red of an oni, she should then put on a red kimono. Next, she should tie her hair up into five "horns" and place an upside-down iron trivet on her head, so that it resembled a crown. Upon the three legs of the stand, she was instructed to tie small pine torches and light them. Finally, she should clench two more torches in her mouth, so that they would hang from either side.

Dressed and arranged in this unique manner, she should imagine herself to be a fiendish oni and walk to the Uji River. Once there, she needed to immerse herself in its water. This must be done for twenty-one nights, then on the final night, her transformation to an oni would be complete and she may visit her husband at his mistress's house and take vengeance.

Meanwhile, her husband was suffering from nightmares. Sensing something terrible was about to happen, he called upon the famous onmyōji (powerful diviner) Abe no Seimei for help. Abe no Seimei also felt the formidable evil that was closing in on the husband. The normally confident Abe no Seimei wasn't sure he could vanquish it, but he promised to try. He had the husband and his lover hide while he constructed two life-sized straw dolls and placed them in their futons. Next, he summoned any god or spirit who could help and used his famed magic to make the straw effigies look like two sleeping lovers.

Later that night, the young woman—carrying a club in one hand—swept into the room like a violent storm. She was now fully transformed into Hashihime. Her kimono blew about her fiery red skin, and her black eyes flashed in the firelight of the small torches burning in her hair. She knelt and whispered her hate into her husband's ear. But before she attacked, she noticed the trick, and turned on Abe no Seimei. The two fought an epic battle of magic in which Hashihime was ultimately defeated and ordered to leave the house. She shrieked in despair at her loss. Then seeing her husband and his lover cowering behind a folding screen, she laughed to herself. This time she'd been overpowered and would not be allowed to exact the revenge she so rightfully deserved. But, before departing, Hashihime looked her husband in the eyes and said:

"You must understand: My resentment will never end. Somewhere, somehow, we will meet again."

Her presence softened, her body turned to mist, and just like that she disappeared.

This story has endured over a thousand years of retelling, all the while splintering off and changing. Hashihime has gone from being a real person, to a demon oni who puts curses on people or tries to kill them, to a protecting spirit who fiercely guards certain bridges and boundaries that have been dedicated to her. This last version of Hashihime is called a mamorigami (守神), or protecting god.

In Modern Stories

The Bridge Princess appears in the manga *Ayashimon* and in *Hashihime of the Old Book Town*, a visual novel game. A visual novel, or VN, is type of digital interactive fiction. There is a clear narrative, either static or animated images, and some kind of interactivity with the story.

NOW YOU KNOW

The Uji Bridge in Kyoto is one of Japan's oldest bridges. Although it has been rebuilt many times, it was originally constructed in C.E. 646. There is a superstition that wedding processions and couples should never cross the bridge. If the spirit of Hashihime sees the happy pair and the beautiful bride, she'll be reminded of what happened over a thousand years ago and fall into a jealous rage. Also, a person should never praise another bridge while they're on one that has been dedicated to Hashihime, as that will also result in a heinous curse befalling them.

HITOTSUME KOZŌ
一つ目小僧

Pronunciation: Hee-TOH-tsoo-may ko-ZOH

Translation: The One-Eyed Boy or One-Eyed Boy Monk

Similar to: Kasa (or Karakasa) Obake (傘お化け);
Chōchin Obake (提灯お化け), and sometimes
mistaken for the Tōfu Kozō (豆腐小僧)

Overview

The hitotsume kozō is one of the sillier yōkai. This mythical beastie looks like a bald boy of about seven to ten years old who wears traditional clothes complete with a straw hat and geta shoes. In some depictions, he looks more like the young monk the latter part of his name, *kozō*, suggests. He might be carrying a paper lantern, a staff, a broom, or nothing at all—oh, and he also has a single unblinking eye in the middle of his face that glows. If you're lucky, you'll encounter one with a lolling tongue as well.

Except for depictions in a few unusual and highly disturbing origin stories, these goofy little fellows aren't evil at all and intend no real harm. It appears that their main life purpose lies in the enjoyment they derive from terrifying unsuspecting fools who unknowingly stumble upon them.

During the Edo era (1603–1867), which was considered the golden age of yōkai, tales abounded about this merry prankster. He could be found hiding in the shadows of some dimly lit street or behind a tree on a lonely path, waiting for the right moment to spring out and scare an innocent passerby.

There are a couple of other yōkai that are similar to hitotsume kozō in terms of appearance and antics. One is the kasa obake (傘お化け), or karakasa obake (which is written with the same kanji characters). This one resembles an old-fashioned paper umbrella with one eye and one leg and has a penchant for hopping around and spooking people. Sometimes it shows off a long dangling tongue too. A few have two arms and, even more rarely, two legs.

Then there's the chōchin obake (提灯お化け), also dubbed the "burabura" by artist Toriyama Sekien. This beast is a time-worn paper lantern with a split across one of its thin bamboo ribs, giving it a mouth, from which hangs that ever-so-ridiculous oversized tongue both the hitotsume kozō and the kasa obake flaunt. The chōchin obake have one-eyed and two-eyed varieties, and they, too, are almost always portrayed as silly goofballs.

Background and Popular Stories

Yanagita Kunio (柳田國男) (1875–1962), the great folklorist who penned *Tōno Monogatari* (遠野物語), or *The Legends of Tono* (1910), proposed that yōkai are fallen gods. He also suggested hitotsume kozō were disgraced mountain deities. This makes sense since some legends mention mountain gods having "crossed eyes." But "crossed eyes" was another way of saying having a single eye.

Another theory put forth by Yanagita Kunio revolves around human sacrifice. In certain communities, when an individual was chosen for this solemn duty, one of their eyes might be intentionally blinded. This served as a way to identify them when the time for the ritual arrived (these rituals sometimes took place as far as one year into the future). Additionally, it was believed that a single-eyed person was more readily able to communicate with the gods. As a result, the selected individual received special treatment and was doted upon throughout the entire period leading up to the final sacrifice.

There is a less divine, less grisly explanation of the one-eyed origin story. In old Japan, iron-smelting accidents were quite common—many who worked in this trade lost an eye in that way. It's possible the one-eyed version of the hitotsume kozō came about because of these poor smelters.

When it comes to the story of the hitotsume kozō, there is a popular rakugo (落語) titled, *Ichigankoku, The One-Eyed Country* (一眼国). (A rakugo, by the way, is a traditional form of comedic storytelling that involves a lone performer on a stage, telling a story using minimal props.) The story goes something like this:

Back when the city of Tokyo was still called Edo, on the grounds of the Ekōin Temple (回向院), exhibitions called misemono (見せ物) were held. These sideshows drew great crowds of people, who gawked at the outrageous spectacles. There were 6-foot-long (2-meter-long) weasels alongside monstrous mermaid mummies and demon girls who ate snakes. All of the more extreme exhibits were, naturally, fake. But the more outlandish something was, the more attention it received, and the more money the sideshow made.

One day the owner, realizing it was just a matter of time before his exhibits were discovered as hoaxes, and fearing loss of credibility, gathered several travelers together. He told them that if they ever come across anything out of the ordinary—anything weird or, better yet, horrific—that he'll add them to his misemono show. He promised that he would pay them handsomely for their information.

One traveler stepped forward. Shivering at the memory, he told the owner about a run-in he'd had on a large plain located north of the city. There he saw an old oak tree, and under it stood a one-eyed girl. He was so shaken by the experience that he fled and tried to erase the memory from his mind.

This was exactly what the sideshow owner was looking for. The next day, he set out for the plain, traveling until dusk; when he finally arrived, he saw the oak tree in the distance. He then heard a girl's voice call out, "Mister! Mister!"

There was the one-eyed girl under the tree! The sideshow owner ran over and scooped her up in his arms, but before he could make any promises of the good life she'd have in the city of Edo, she began screaming. All at once, sounds rang throughout the plain: bamboo flutes whistled, bells rung, drums were beaten. He heard a horde of people racing toward him.

The sideshow owner put the girl back down and ran. But the mob quickly gained on him and he collapsed on the ground, cowering as the mob surrounded him.

"Where are you from?" the lead authority demanded. "Do you realize that kidnapping is a crime?"

The sideshow owner glanced up. To his horror, every single person who had gathered around him had only one eye! He quickly looked back down in fear.

"Look at me when I'm talking!" the authority shouted. "Raise your face!"

"Raise your face!" the mob chanted.

The sideshow owner did, and the crowd gasped.

"He's a monster!" said a voice. "He has two eyes!"

"We'll investigate his crimes later," the authority said. "Quick! Let's put him in our sideshow!"

In Modern Stories

Hitotsume kozō appears in products from the Japanese media franchise *Yo-kai Watch* as well as in *GeGeGe no Kitarō* and is Kyororo in *Super Mario Land 2*. He's also a character in the open-world action role-playing game *Genshin Impact*. In all of these, he doesn't deviate from the straw-hat-wearing, one-eyed boy sticking his tongue out.

ITTAN MOMEN
一反木綿

Pronunciation: EE-tahn MOH-men

Translation: One Length of Cotton Cloth

Etymology: Cloth used to be measured in units called *tan*
in Japan. One *tan*, or *ittan* (一反), is about 35 feet (10.6 meters)
in length and 12 inches (30 centimeters) in width.
Momen (木綿) is the word for cotton.

Also known as: Ittan Monme (いったんもんめ)

Similar to: Futon Kabuse (布団被せ); Fusuma (衾);
Nodeppō (野鉄砲), meaning "improvised gun"

Overview

The ittan momen is an affable-enough-looking yōkai. It's a long, narrow bolt
of white cotton that flaps around or flies deftly through the air. But it's not as
innocent as it looks. The ittan momen is said to swoop in, wrap itself around
some unwitting individual's neck and face, and in a worst-case scenario, suf-
focate them. Other accounts have it enveloping its victim's entire body and
whisking them away into the sky.

The legend of these attacking airborne pieces of cloth first came from
Kagoshima Prefecture, Kyushu (specifically, the Kimotsuki District). There

is a shrine, named Shijūkusho Jinja (四十九諸神社), where reports of the ittan momen's ominous presence can still be felt as of today.

Surprisingly, the ittan momen wasn't illustrated by artist Toriyama Sekien, who envisioned so many of the yōkai and other creatures we know and love (or fear) today. But there is a scroll dating before Sekien's woodblock books called the *Daitokuji Shinjuan* (大徳寺真珠庵) or the *Hyakki Yagyō Emaki* (百鬼夜行絵巻), which translates to something like *Illustrated Scroll of the Nocturnal Procession of One Hundred Demons*.

In it, there are a couple of creatures hiding underneath large, billowing cloths, with only the tips of their clawed feet visible. Folklorist Komatsu Kazuhiko supposes that these early images, while not ittan momen per se, might have been the genesis for the eventual yōkai that terrorized oblivious travelers.

Background and Popular Stories

Stories of this flying fabric were passed down locally for years, but it wasn't until Mizuki Shigeru added the ittan momen character to his beloved manga and anime series *GeGeGe no Kitarō* that the yōkai gained popularity.

Mizuki Shigeru took the liberty to further anthropomorphize the monster and, in the process, give it a much-needed makeover. He provided little flaps of cloth for arms and two slits for eyes, and gave it the very distinctive accent from its native Kagoshima. He also turned the fluttering beastie from the original fierce—and potentially deadly—monster into the main character Kitarō's friend and also transformed it into a reliable method of high-speed air travel.

There are three other yōkai that resemble the ittan momen, but with their own unique, quirky differences: the futon kabuse (布団被せ), the fusuma (衾), and the nodeppō (野鉄砲). The futon kabuse behaves most like the ittan momen, but instead of a thin bolt of cloth, it's a large, heavy futon (suffocation ensues).

The fusuma is named after a Heian-era (C.E. 794–1185) type of bedding that looks like a quilt. However, this one is so strong, no blade can harm it. At least not at first. It's said that it can eventually be cut up, but only by someone who has blackened their teeth at least once and makes a tear on it with those same teeth. Then it can be sliced to shreds. Teeth blackening—a process called ohaguro (お歯黒)—was once a common practice in Japan among married women (and, at different times, younger children and even men). It involved a particularly foul concoction of iron acetate, vinegar, sake, strong tea, and tannic acid powder made from the gallnuts of a Japanese sumac tree. It was believed to be beautiful and was done to indicate status and to protect one's teeth. This practice continued for centuries before it was outlawed by the Meiji government in 1870.

The final ittan momen–related yōkai is the nodeppō. Its name means "handmade gun" or "wild gun," which will make sense in a minute. The nodeppō does not bear any physical resemblance to the ittan momen; it looks more like a flying tanuki (Japanese raccoon dog) or flying squirrel. But like the ittan momen, the nodeppō lives deep in the forest and valleys; it also has the propensity to fly down and attach itself to a random victim to either asphyxiate or, in some cases, exsanguinate them.

The nodeppō also does something a little extra: It shoots a stream of bat-like creatures from its mouth. These creatures fly down and cover the target's face, but instead of smothering them, they steal the person's food while they're distracted.

It's interesting to note that there is a giant flying squirrel called a musasabi (ムササビ) that is indigenous to Japan. These animals can sometimes look like pieces of square cloths when they spread their limbs to take flight; they are also known to land on your face and hold on. This might explain the ittan momen, the futon kabuse, the fusuma, and the nodeppō to some extent. (It doesn't shed any light on the creature firing bats from its maw, though.)

One unusual encounter with an ittan momen goes like this: A man was hurrying home after dark when suddenly a white cloth flew down and wrapped itself around his face and neck. He struggled but he could not tear it off. Remembering his short sword, he used it to carefully slice through the offending material. That did the trick. But after he returned home, he noticed there was blood on his hands.

In Modern Stories

Ittan momen appear in *GeGeGe no Kitarō* as well as in the game *Ghostwire: Tokyo*, where there's actually a mission called "Ittan-momen." In the game, you have to capture one of the nastier varieties. They also show up in the game *Onmyoji*, where they are depicted as flying women with undulating robes.

JINMENJU, JINMENKEN, AND JINMENGYO

人面樹, 人面犬, and 人面魚

Pronunciation: JEEN-men-joo, JEEN-men-ken, and JEEN-men-gyoh

Etymology: The two characters representing *jin men* mean "human" and "face," or "human-faced." The final character in each word means "tree," "dog," and "fish," in that order. So, these mean "human-faced tree," "human-faced dog," and "human-faced fish."

Overview

In Japan, you'll find some human-faced yōkai that, quite disturbingly, shouldn't possess human features at all, such as the jinmenju (human-faced tree), the jinmenken (human-faced dog), and the jinmengyo (human-faced fish). These entities exist primarily to give you a fright.

An ill-fated stroll alone at night could very well have you meeting all three. For instance, say you're walking along an arched stone bridge in a Japanese garden and paused to gaze down at the pond. In the moonlight, which seems to feed your already overactive imagination, you might notice that among the koi swimming near the surface of the water, one looks like it has the face of a man. That would be a jinmengyo.

Startled, you look away, but that tree over there, the one with the branches heavy with fruit, also looks curious. It's almost as if each piece of fruit has a pair of eyes, a nose, and a mouth and is smiling at you, giggling! That is a jinmenju.

You hear a noise and jump. You're relieved to see only a dog trotting your way. It actually feels better knowing you're not entirely alone. You reach down to give it a pet on the head when suddenly, it looks up at you, and you're staring into the eyes of an elderly man. Meet the jinmenken.

Background and Popular Stories

Of these three bizarre creatures, the jinmenju is the oldest. Not only was it included in Toriyama Sekien's *Konjaku Hyakki Shūi* (今昔百機種位), or *Supplement to the Hundred Demons from the Present and the Past* (1781), it also goes further back, appearing in an older 105-volume illustrated encyclopedia published in 1712 called the *Wakan Sansai Zue* (和漢三才図会), which translates to *Illustrated Sino-Japanese Encyclopedia*.

Within this expansive tome, encompassing subjects ranging from natural history and astronomy to accounts of strange and different lands, there is a mention of the Daishikoku (大食国), literally "big-eat country," but referred to as the "Land of Gluttony," located in a faraway southwestern land. In the descriptions of this mythical place, we find the possible origins of the human-faced tree. There is an entry that mentions flowers with human heads that laugh when asked questions but don't seem to understand human language. If they laugh too much, though, they wither and drop to the ground. Other stories of the jinmenju assert that depending on the character of the spirit inhabiting the tree, some are actually able to express emotion and speak.

In Toriyama Sekien's woodblock print, he shows the jinmenju as blossoms that take the form of little bald human heads (Sekien called them ninmenju, using a different pronunciation for the first character). But if you look way back, you'll find these face fruits actually derive from very old tales and have been traced to Indian and Persian legends.

The jinmenken, or human-faced dog, is a much more recent yōkai or urban legend. It gained attention from 1989–1990 among elementary and junior high school students, with sightings of jinmenken running at incredible speeds, passing cars, then turning to look back at the drivers, revealing their faces and causing accidents. Other urban legends allege that man-faced canines were spotted rummaging through garbage cans. When confronted, they'd mumble, "Hottoite kure!" or "Leave me alone!" For the most part, these blended dogs just want their privacy.

Finally, there is the jinmengyo, the human-faced fish. Similar to the jinmenken, this human-beast hybrid surfaced in the 1990s when the tabloid *Friday* published a photo of a purported jinmengyo sent in by a reader. It was said to be taken in Tsuruoka City, Yamagata Prefecture, at a small lake near the temple Zenpōji (善法寺). Some people wonder if jinmengyo could have surfaced because some unique koi have markings on the tops of their heads that are eerily similar to human faces, sometimes even with mustaches or beards. Looking down into a koi pond and spotting one can be disconcerting, as at first glance, it looks like there is a face staring up at you from under the water.

A superstition has arisen around jinmengyo too. Reminiscent of yōkai of old—like the mermaids and the amabie—it is said to do some portending. Some old wives' tales state that if one appears, it means a tsunami is coming. This is echoed in the Studio Ghibli movie *Ponyo* (2008), in which Ponyo herself is a kind of jinmengyo, with her fish body and little girl head. In the Japanese version of the movie, when the elderly women first see Ponyo, one actually says that when a jinmengyo emerges from the ocean, a tsunami is imminent.

An alternate take on the human-faced animal is another more recent yōkai called the nekomengyo, or cat-faced fish. There's an interesting legend about this one-off modern yōkai as well.

Once upon a time, on the Gongen Mountain near Ibuki Falls in Gifu Prefecture, there lived a large menacing cat that measured nearly 6 feet (1.8 meters) long. (Perhaps it was a nekomata? See the Bakeneko and Nekomata entry.) Its favorite food were the koi that lived in the bottom of the pond at Ibuki Falls. But this feared feline was so big and slow, it couldn't catch them very well.

One day, the cat pleaded to the water god (was it a dragon?—see the Ryū entry), "I wish to be able to eat enough koi so that I become full." Surprisingly, the water god answered, "Okay, but if you wish to eat to your heart's content, then you must be able to swim. I will grant your wish by leaving your face like that of a cat but changing your body into a fish."

The cat thought this was a marvelous idea and after the change, immediately jumped into the lake. Only, once it touched the water, its appetite for fish completely vanished. This nekomengyo proved to be very adaptable. Soon it became friends with the other fish, and to this day, it lives peacefully there with its fish buddies.

Some people say, though, that on certain nights, you can see a cat-faced fish walking—yes, walking!—around the area.

In Modern Stories

It's easy to spot the Pokémon that is based off the human-faced tree—Exeggutor. *Yo-kai Watch* has a human-faced dog in it, and as for the human-faced fish, there is the 1999 game *Seaman*, where you raise your own virtual pet, a jinmengyo called the Gillman. One unique feature the Gillman has is a small tube on the top of its head. At some stage in the game, it attacks other human-faced fish and drinks their blood through this tube. It will also talk to you.

NOW YOU KNOW

Scholar and collector of rare books and trivia Ishizuka Hōkaishi wrote that on April 29, 1819, a puppy born near Nihonbashi in Edo (now Tokyo) had a humanlike face. According to some accounts, its face actually more resembled that of a monkey, but its front paws did look human-ish.

JINMENSŌ

人面瘡

Pronunciation: JEEN-men-soh

Translation: The Human-Faced "Tumor"

Similar to: Jinmenju (人面樹), Human-Faced Tree;
Jinmenken (人面犬), Human-Faced Dog;
and Jinmengyo (人面魚) Human-Faced Fish

Overview

The jinmensō is probably one of the most unsettling yōkai you'll ever meet—or, more precisely, become afflicted with. It isn't a creepy beastie you can battle or run away from; instead, it is a growth that mysteriously appears on some part of your body and doesn't go away. What makes it a yōkai is that, somewhere along the line, you'll notice it has a face and can eat, drink, and even occasionally talk.

The earliest mention of this grotesque malady can be found in ancient Chinese texts. But there are also Japanese medical documents from the 1800s that are queasily specific when talking about this parasitic beast. For example, one medical record dated July 1819 describes a thirty-five-year-old merchant in Sendai who came in to be examined for a suspicious-looking growth on his knee. It had been there since he was fourteen years old. Every year, it had grown in size, but it wasn't until that day in July that he finally decided to do something about it.

The doctor recorded the affliction in gruesome detail. He wrote that the mysterious bump had swollen parts that looked like a smiling face, with a pale red mouth, two nostrils, and closed eyes. It even had ears. The physician then went on to say that if he touched it, it would bleed, but that the patient experienced no pain. But that's not all. The little beast also twitched, which made it look like it was breathing. Although, to his credit, he noted this could have been the man's heartbeat (or pulse) making it look like it was respiring.

The doctor's diagnosis was that because it looked so much like a human face, it must be an akuryō (悪霊) or onryō (怨霊), the evil spirit of someone (dead or alive) who had so much malice directed toward the victim, it manifested itself in this way.

Background and Popular Stories

It's important to note a slight mistranslation you'll often see, that a jinmensō is a "human-faced tumor." That's not quite right. The last kanji sō (瘡) is the same character used in the word for smallpox. It means "pustule" or "boil" and refers to any kind of sore that erupts on the skin. So, it's not exactly a tumor.

Back in the mid-1600s, an author and monk named Asai Ryōi wrote about this phenomenon in his bizarre collection of sixty-five short stories entitled *Otogibōko*. The stories in this book are mostly adapted from Chinese and Korean texts, with Asai Ryōi altering and embellishing them as he desired. The story about the human-faced pustule appeared in volume 9 and was titled "Jinmensō."

The story chronicles a farmer, living in what is now the city of Uji in Kyoto, who fell very ill and wasn't able to recover. Six months after he got sick, he noticed he had an incredibly painful, strange growth on his knee. He examined it closer and was startled to find it had eyes and a mouth and resembled a human face. Was it a jinmensō? He dismissed it as a weird coincidence and went about his usual routine.

However, a little while later, he was at home, drinking to try to numb the pain this peculiar boil caused, when—feeling a little tipsy, no doubt—he poured a bit of sake onto the jinmensō. To his astonishment, the tiny mouth drank it up. Not only that, but after several gulps, the creepy yōkai flushed red as some do when they get drunk. This made the farmer more curious. He pulled off a tiny piece of mochi rice cake from a plate on the table and fed it to his enthusiastic knee cyst. Horrified, the farmer watched as the tiny mouth chewed up and swallowed the sticky treat.

This was the beginning of a change in the farmer and his jinmensō's relationship. The parasitic yōkai was painful enough as it was, but now, if the poor man didn't feed it, the ache would quickly become unbearable. So, every day he would have to feed the dreadful beast, and every day it would demand more. It wasn't long before the farmer was sacrificing his own meals and started wasting away.

He tried to get help. He visited different doctors and healers around town, but no one had a solution to his problem. Mostly they were just grossed out. Meanwhile, the farmer was slowly starving to death.

Then one day when all was at its worst, a wandering ascetic monk (ascetics were monks who deprived themselves of comforts and pleasures) happened to visit the town. He heard about the tormented man's dilemma and offered his help. He told him to sell all his land for gold, then use that money to buy specific medicines and herbs. What could he do? This was his last hope. The farmer agreed and did as directed.

After he'd acquired the needed treatments, the monk went to the farmer's house and fed the remedies to the jinmensō one by one, noting the reactions. But there was no effect. It would just gobble them up and cry out for more. This went on for some time, until finally the monk tried to place some powdered baimo(貝母), or snake's head fritillary (a type of lily) into the creature's maw. The previously voracious jinmensō suddenly closed its mouth tight and refused to eat.

"Aha!" the monk said, and force-fed the powdered flower to the mouth. Almost immediately, the farmer felt better. After seventeen days, the swelling went down, the mysterious growth disappeared, and the farmer recovered entirely.

In Modern Stories

The jinmensō shows up in the manga *The Kurosagi Corpse Delivery Service*, written by Eiji Otsuka, with art by Hosui Yamazaki; the manga has an English-language adaption published by Dark Horse Comics. The jinmensō also made somewhat of a TV debut back in March 2022. After my podcast *Uncanny Japan* did an episode on this repulsive little monster, one month later, *Saturday Night Live* did a sketch called "Meatballs," which was about a woman afflicted with several eating, singing, and vomiting round growths all over her body. It could have been a coincidence, but it's fun to think this gross little yōkai now has an American cousin.

JORŌGUMO

絡新婦 or 女郎蜘蛛

Pronunciation: JOH-roh-GOO-moh

Translation: The Harlot Spider or Entangling Bride

Overview

The jorōgumo is a creepy, potentially deadly yōkai who has two different embodiments and two different ways of writing her name, depending on which form she's inhabiting. Both names are pronounced exactly the same way, though.

If you run across her as a beautiful, beguiling woman hanging out in or near a waterfall, the characters (絡新婦) mean "entangling bride." If, on the other hand, she's a giant spider who has captured you with a sticky thread and is luring you in for your ultimate demise, the kanji (女郎蜘蛛) mean "harlot spider."

The famed woodblock artist Toriyama Sekien used both names. For the title of her page in his classic collection *Gazu Hyakki Yagyō* (画図百鬼夜行), or *Illustrated Demon Horde's Night Parade* (1776), he chose the "entangling bride" characters, while in the table of contents, he went with "harlot spider." A close look at his image also shows something in between the two forms. In this early depiction, you see what looks like the back of a long-haired, kimono-clad woman, then you notice she has six spider legs protruding from those silken robes (she's standing on the other two). What's even more startling is that on the end of every one of those hairy appendages is a fire-breathing baby spider seemingly being whipped about in the air. (It's a shame that these days, you don't often hear mention of fire-breathing baby spiders in relation to the jorōgumo.)

Background and Popular Stories

The spider woman's origins date back hundreds of years ago when there were gorgeous waterfalls flowing into crystal-clear pools all across the country, untouched by human hands and unseen by human eyes. These were magical places where large spiders lived and acted as messengers for the water deities. Over time, travelers started wandering close to these falls and it was discovered these jumbo arachnids also had the power—if they were so inclined—to change into enchanting women.

In order to safeguard these sacred places from intruders, the jorōgumo would shoot out gluey webs, entrapping them. It wasn't long before the cascades where these spider women resided came to be known as "spider pools," or—because the women used their spare time and their spider silks to weave—"weaving pools." If you're ever out in the wilderness of Japan and come across a waterfall, listen closely for the sound of a loom. If you hear it, you might not want to stick around.

These jorōgumo weren't necessarily out to entangle and kill innocent men, however. Remember, they were messengers for the water deities, and it was the men who trespassed into *their* territory.

When one of these spiders decided to transform into a woman, she appeared as the most bewitchingly beautiful lady the man had ever seen. Her allure was so potent that once he saw her, her seductive beauty was etched into his memory forever.

If, though, he discovered her true identity, the spider lady would demand that the man keep it a secret. This is where problems arose. Trying to silence those who had fallen under her spell was itself a trick. The following is a well-known story about just such a case.

Once upon a time, at Jōren Falls in Izu, Shizuoka Prefecture, there lived a jorōgumo. This came to light when one day a man was resting beside the bank of the plunge pool when a web shot out from the water, wrapped around his leg, and started to drag him in. This particular fellow was a quick thinker, though, and deftly pulled off the sticky webbing, winding it around a nearby tree stump instead. He then watched as the stump was uprooted and pulled into the waterfall.

From that time on, no one dared go near the place—until one day, when a woodcutter visiting the area for the first time found himself at the breathtaking falls. While there, he suddenly had the urge to chop down a tree with his axe. As he was doing so, he accidentally dropped his favorite tool into the water. He was just about to dive in after it when the most captivating woman he'd ever seen emerged from the water with it in her hands and returned it to him.

He thanked her, and she made him swear never to tell anyone that he had met her here. If he did, she warned, it would cost him his life. He promised and quickly left the area.

The man then stopped by the nearby town, and without telling anyone about his own experience, he learned that a jorōgumo did indeed live at Jōren Falls. Now he understood fully the danger and kept their meeting locked inside his heart. Years went by, and he never said a word, but he often remembered that day and very much wished he was able to tell someone about it.

Finally, while out drinking with his friends one night, he could hold it in no longer. He let slip what had occurred that fateful day. As soon as he did, the burden he had been carrying around for years was lifted, and his heart felt lighter. That night, he went to bed feeling happy and content for the first time in ages, only, he never woke up again.

There are some alternate endings to this oft-told story of Jōren Falls. One is that after the woodcutter revealed the spider woman's secret, an invisible thread pulled him outside, and he walked off into the night. Later he was found floating in the same pool where he'd met the jorōgumo years before.

In Modern Stories

Jorōgumo can be found in a ton of manga, anime, and games. In the manga and anime *Demon Slayer*, a version of her is shown as Rui's mother, an all-white spider lady who controls others with her sticky threads. In *One Piece*, she appears as Black Maria, a giant blonde-haired beauty. A few other manga and anime she's in are *Inuyasha*, *xxxHOLiC*, and *Yo-kai Watch*. The character Rakna-Kadaki in the game *Monster Hunter: Rise* is based on the jorōgumo, with her webbing made to look like a wedding dress in reference to the version of her name that means "entangling bride." She can breathe fire too, just like the little baby spiders in Sekien's iconic image.

NOW YOU KNOW

The jorōgumo is not just a mythic eight-legged femme fatale—it is also an actual spider in Japan. These spiders are a type of golden orb weaver native to Asia, but they have managed to stow away in shipping containers in recent years and have arrived in North America. The females are large and quite attractive, with bright yellow, green, and red markings. These jorōgumo spiders are harmless to humans, but they will put some hurt on the stink bug population if given a chance.

KAMAITACHI

鎌鼬

Pronunciation: KAH-mah-EE-tah-chee

Translation: The Sickle Weasel

Etymology: The two characters literally mean "sickle" and "weasel," and they refer not only to the type of cut the beast gives people but also to the fact that it looks like a weasel with sickles on its paws.

Also known as: Iizuna (飯綱) in eastern Aichi Prefecture

Overview

The kamaitachi is another elusive and dangerous—but ultimately nondeadly—yōkai. It's a beast that moves so fast, you can't even see it; some rumors say it might just be invisible. Despite that, its likeness was captured by Toriyama Sekien in the eponymously titled woodblock print "Kamaitachi" found in *Gazu Hyakki Yagyō* (画図百鬼夜行), or *Illustrated Demon Horde's Night Parade* (1776).

Here, he carved an image of a weasel-looking creature, its front paw blades brandished, in the center of a whirlwind. It's unclear whether the animal kicked up that tempest all by itself or is just riding in on it. While descriptions and artistic renditions of this yōkai are mostly similar, its method of attack can vary wildly depending on regional differences. For example, the kamaitachi might ride in suddenly on a gust of wind, or it might choose to sneak up on you, without any change to the weather. As it creeps up on you, the kamaitachi might decide to knock you off your feet—or, you might think nothing happened at all, until you notice the injury on your body.

It's the laceration that all kamaitachi attacks have in common. At some point, you'll discover a cut or cuts on your skin, usually on the lower part of your body—calves, shins, and thighs—that you have no memory of getting. Typically, it doesn't hurt, and there is little to no bleeding. Some think the reason why there is no blood is because the little fur devils swoop in and suck it all away, leaving a clean wound. Mysteriously, the cut or cuts can be on exposed skin or covered skin.

These kamaitachi stories mostly hail from the Yamanashi, Nagano, and Niigata regions—places that all have harsh winters. The extreme cold seems to have something to do with the cuts. But strikes from the beast have been reported from all over the country.

Background and Popular Stories

There is a Chinese mythical creature called a kyūki (窮奇), which is considered one of four "bad luck beasts," or shikyō (四凶); this creature may have been an origin for the kamaitachi. The kyūki is said to either have the body of an ox, the hide of a hedgehog, a bark like a dog, and an appetite for people or to be a winged tiger with long-bladed claws that also eats people, although this one consumes them from the head down. This creature is also classified as a wind god that wields the power to manipulate the wind and possesses knives for claws. You can see the similarities it has with the kamaitachi, which came later. It's interesting, though, that the completely different kanji characters for *kyūki* can still be read as "kamaitachi."

Another theory posits that the kamaitachi isn't a single yōkai but a trio of evil gods called akugami (悪神). The first one knocks you down, the second one slashes you with a blade, and the third one applies magical ointment to the wound so it doesn't bleed or hurt.

An interesting theory about the origin of the name *kamaitachi* is that it's a pun or a play on the characters *kamae* and *tachi* (構え and 太刀). *Kamae* means to "get ready for a fight" or "get into your fighting stance," and *tachi* means "sword." A tachi is different than a katana (a traditional Japanese sword with a distinctive single-edged blade and a long grip for holding with both hands) and was in fact invented first. It has a more pronounced curvature and was worn with the blade facing down, whereas a katana faces up. The wounds that the kamaitachi inflicts look very similar to slashes you'd get if struck by a tachi's blade.

Another hypothesis is that the name comes from *kaze no ma* (風の間), meaning "the space between the wind," which alludes to the incredible speed at which a kamaitachi attacks.

Most of the stories of encounters with kamaitachi are (ahem) cut-and-dry. There is one, however, that is quite out of the ordinary. It goes something like this:

Once upon a time, in Ōme City, Tokyo, there was a woman whose lover left her for another. She was devastated. In her grief, she cut off all her long hair. Without delay, the chopped-off locks turned themselves into a kamaitachi, flew to the other woman's home, and exacted revenge by slicing off her head in a single stroke.

This head lopper offer aside, kamaitachi are usually nonlethal. You will discover, though, that with quite a few of the more playful mythical beasties in Japan, there are often one or two tales with a much more sinister slant. It is sometimes in the original tale and sometimes evolves in the retelling.

In Modern Stories

The kamaitachi sneakily appears in the manga and anime *Naruto*, where the character Temari, a wind user, has a special technique that summons a kamaitachi. In the anime version of *One Piece*, there is magical fruit called the Kama Kama no Mi (meaning "Sickle-Sickle Fruit"), which, once eaten, will give the person long, sharp sickle-like nails for fighting or slicing through hard objects like rocks. Of course, there are some Pokémon that are based off this speedy yōkai, such as Sneasel, Sneasler, Weavile, and the one simply named Kamaitachi. Finally, a wind attack dubbed "Kamaitachi" is one of the Geomancer skills in the *Final Fantasy* game.

NOW YOU KNOW

Some believe the wound left by the kamaitachi could be a very real condition caused by a change of air pressure. A sudden shift in the barometric pressure brought along by a whirlwind and cold air can cause the plumper parts of your body to split open. There's another hypothesis that suggests sudden gusts of wind carrying small stones or other debris whoosh in and inflict the injuries. However, this wouldn't explain how you can get them on your skin even if you're all bundled up.

KAPPA
河童

Pronunciation: KAH-pah

Translation: The River Child or Water Goblin

Also known as: Kawatarō (川太郎), Gawappa (ガワッパ),
Komahiki (駒引き), horse puller; Suiko (水虎),
water tiger; Enko (エンコ)

Overview

Kappa are some of the better-known yōkai in Japan and, more recently, all over the world. But these scrawny, child-sized water-dwelling beasties have been prowling the lakes, rivers, ponds, swamps, and oceans of Japan for more than a thousand years. But they haven't always looked the same.

Over time, the kappa has assumed various appearances. In ancient stories and artwork, you'll see it depicted as a monkey-like beast, a soft-shelled turtle, and even an otter. However, in contemporary sources, this river child is often categorized into two main types: One, originating in western Japan, is a hairy, simian, shell-less creature. The other, from eastern Japan, is much more prevalent and popular. It is about the size of a three- to ten-year-old child and is covered in scales or slimy froggy skin and possesses webbed hands and feet. It has a parrot-like beak on its face, a tortoise shell on its back, and a saucer-like indentation on the top of its head that holds strength-giving water. The depression is surrounded by a mussed-up ring of bristly hair. Its skin color is typically green these days, but in older texts, it is said to have a red face and yellow eyes. Then there is the smell.

One thing all kappa have in common is their aroma. Kappa are said to reek. It's not just their normal fishy odor you have to worry about, though—their flatulence is rumored to be so vile it can cause instant death.

The earliest mention of a kappa-like creature can be found in the *Nihon Shoki*, which was written around C.E. 720. This book describes something called a mizuchi, or "water snake," living in the Kahashima River in what is now eastern Hiroshima. This brute not only harassed passersby, it killed a whole bunch as well.

The mizuchi continued to bother and even murder people until one brave soul finally confronted the water beast. After threatening it for a while, the man tossed some gourds into the water and posed a challenge. If the mizuchi could sink them, then the man would leave it alone so—we can deduce—it could proceed with its reign of terror on the community. If the mizuchi couldn't hold the gourds under the water, though, the man would then slay the monster and cut it up into pieces. As it turns out, for as strong and deadly as the mizuchi was, it was easily thwarted by the task of trying to submerge a gourd.

Background and Popular Stories

Originally, these aquatic yōkai were extremely dangerous, heinous creatures that lurked in or near water, waiting to drown oblivious swimmers or (arguably worse) reach in to yank out the mysterious shirikodama (尻子玉)—a small mythical ball that was supposedly located inside a person's rectum. Removing it also caused death.

If they weren't drowning you or stealing your shirikodama, these water goblins were inviting you to wrestle, sumo-style. It was an invitation you couldn't refuse, but you had no chance of winning either. Kappa are made

inordinately strong by the water they keep in their skull saucers. But lucky for you, despite their overall vileness, they aren't completely without manners. The key to defeating one, if you don't have a gourd handy, is to politely bow deeply to your kappa opponent before the match. It will bow in return, thus draining the water from its head and weakening it. A couple other sure-fire kappa deterrents are: iron, ginger, and saliva. These days, fortunately, kappa have undergone a transformation into a more adorable, whimsical, and much less menacing persona.

Kappa absolutely adore eggplants, melons, soba noodles, natto (fermented soybeans), pumpkins, and cucumbers. They are especially enthusiastic about those little yellow flowers you can sometimes find on the ends of cucumbers. But when those tiny blossoms are hard to find, the cucumber itself remains the kappa's favorite food. In some areas of Japan, parents used to give offerings of cucumbers to the local kappa, begging that it not hurt their child, as children often played in rivers and were easy targets. These green gifts were either left at shrines, placed on the banks of rivers and lakes, or thrown into the water itself. To identify which little ones to steer clear of, parents sometimes carved the names and ages of their children into the flesh of the vegetable before offering it. Kappas' fondness for cucumbers can still be seen today if you're familiar with sushi. A cucumber roll in Japanese is called a kappa maki.

Tales about kappas usually involve some cruel prank, such as pulling a farmer's horse or cow into a river, but then it gets caught and pleads for mercy. Forgiveness is finally given—but only after the kappa promises to teach some mysterious medicine or obscure practice of bone setting.

Here's one such story. Once, a woman was visiting the outhouse at night when, out of the darkness of the toilet, a webbed hand reached up and touched her backside. Angry and appalled, the next night she returned armed with a knife. When the hand reached up as it had before, she lopped it off and carried it inside to show it to her husband. The following evening, a one-armed kappa appeared at their door, imploring them to return its limb so it could reattach it. The couple refused. This exchange went on for three nights, until the desperate kappa promised to never do any more mischief and also to share knowledge of crafting a secret medicine capable of healing injuries and mending bones.

In Modern Stories

You might have first seen or read about the more horrific version of the kappa in *Harry Potter and the Prisoner of Azkaban* and also in *Fantastic Beasts and Where to Find Them*. For a more harmless example of the kappa, think about the character Kapp'n in *Animal Crossing*. In the English edition of the game, it's said to be a green turtle, but look at that spiky hairdo, its skull bowl, and its name—Kapp'n is indeed a kappa. Let's not forget the Pokémon who share kappa traits: Lotad, Lombre, Ludicolo, and Capsakid. These days in Japan, kappa images can be found on signs near rivers warning swimmers to be careful or not to litter.

> ### NOW YOU KNOW
>
> Remember that kappa are flatulent? Well, there's a saying in Japan: "he no kappa" (屁の河童), or more recently, "kappa no he" (河童の屁), which literally means "a kappa's fart." In this case, the phrase isn't referring to the creature's foul odor, but instead it indicates something that is extremely easy to do. In English, you would say, "piece of cake."

KINTARŌ

金太郎

Pronunciation: KEEN-tah-roh

Translation: The Golden Boy

Etymology: *Kin* means "gold," "money," or "metal."
Tarō used to be a popular name for first-born boys.

Overview

Kintarō isn't a beastly, harmful, or playful yōkai but instead a much-beloved folkloric hero who goes by "Golden Boy" in the west. He is known for his incredible strength. Even as a child, he romped around the mountains in his scant attire, smashing rocks, uprooting trees, and wrestling bears, sumo-style. He was almost always in the company of his animal friends—a bear, a rabbit, a monkey, and a giant carp—sometimes riding them, sometimes fighting them, oftentimes going on adventures with them. It is rumored he had the ability to talk to them as well.

Kintarō's epic exploits can be found not only in folktales and children's books but also in numerous pieces of art by such masters as Utagawa Kuniyoshi (1798–1861), Utagawa Kunimaru (1794–1829), Kitagawa Utamaro (1753–1806), and Tsukioka Yoshitoshi (1839–1892), to name a few. It's always easy to spot Kintarō. He's red skinned, plump, and naked, or nearly so. You'll also find him sporting a bob haircut with the very top shaved, perhaps symbolizing his warrior spirit, as that is how samurai wore their hair, to keep their heads cool inside their helmets. He also carries a battle-axe and, when not completely in the buff, wears a diamond-shaped red bib with the character for gold, *kin* (金)—the first kanji in his name—written on it.

Kintarō statues and figurines are popular to give to little boys to display around May 5, a day that was named after the ceremony Tango no Sekku (端午の節句) and called Boy's Day (girls have their own day on March 3, called Hina Matsuri (ひな祭り), or the Doll Festival.). The fifth of May celebrated boys and their parents' wishes that they grow up healthy and strong, just like Kintarō. In 1948, the Japanese government officially changed the holiday's name to Kodomo no Hi (こどもの日), or Children's Day. But it still retains the spirit of Tango no Sekku.

Background and Popular Stories

Of the three big mythical folk heroes in Japan (see the Momotarō and Urashima Tarō entries for the other two), Kintarō has the most historical facts connected to his story. He's also the only one who doesn't have a single folktale that can be easily retold over and over. Instead, there are many fragments of legends from his exceptional life that have been passed down and elaborated on.

Kintarō didn't always go by that distinct and lauded name. He was born Sakata Kaidōmaru (坂田怪童丸) and seems to be based on a real person. Later, he went by the moniker Sakata no Kintoki (坂田金時) and was a powerful warrior who lived during the Heian era (C.E. 794–1185) and served as a retainer (loyal follower) to the great samurai Minamoto no Yorimitsu (源頼光) (C.E. 948–1021), who sometimes went by Minamoto no Raikō.

While this superhuman character's adult adventures are incredible and talked about a little elsewhere in this book, it's the mythical childhood adventures of Kintarō that have boosted this chubby little champion to the status of one of Japan's most cherished folk heroes.

There are numerous legends of his birth. They usually start with him being born in May of c.e. 956. From here the narratives veer into different directions. Some tales describe his mother as a woman named Yaegiri who loved him dearly and raised him well. In others, she had to flee after some family infighting and raised him in the forests on Mount Ashigara as well as she could. There are also versions where Yaegiri dies soon after their escape, leaving Kintarō an orphan. The parentless Kintarō might also have been raised by a yamauba, or mountain witch.

Other variants of the story state that Yaegiri (or the yamauba) was impregnated by a thunderclap, making Kintarō's father Raijin (雷神), the god of thunder. This would explain his extraordinary strength. But there is also speculation that Kintarō's father was a red dragon, which would account for his reddish skin. Although, usually, the rosy color is attributed to him being healthy and full of vigor.

A common Kintarō folktale goes like this: Long ago, in the forests on Mount Ashigara, the baby Kintarō lived with his doting mother. The legendary babe was an unusually strong child, and by the time he was crawling, he was able to pull a large millstone behind him. Praying for him to grow up bigger and stronger, his mother embroidered a bib with the first character of his name on it—*kin*, meaning "metal," "gold," or "money."

When he grew older, the little boy was still indefatigable and spent most of his days outside playing with the animals that he had befriended and showing off his incredible strength, usually by challenging them to bouts of sumo, which he always won.

One day, a large bear lumbered by and challenged him, saying, "You might be strong, but you're no match for me." Kintarō accepted the challenge. The other animals acted as referees while the two wrestled. But the match didn't last long, as Kintarō easily defeated the bear.

But there were no hard feelings. The two became fast friends, and Kintarō could be seen riding his new buddy through the woods on his different adventures, such as while collecting chestnuts or fighting demon ogres.

Kintarō became Sakata no Kintoki (or Sakata Kintoki) at the age of twenty, when he met Minamoto no Yorimitsu and, impressing the great leader with his might, was invited to become a retainer for the samurai, completing the famous fighting foursome Shitennō (四天王), or Four Heavenly Kings. Later, they were the ones who defeated Japan's most heinous oni, Shuten Dōji, and the dreaded giant spider the tsuchigumo.

Kintoki's death was quite anticlimactic after such a thrilling life. His master, Yorimitsu, died, and Kintoki spent three months visiting his grave every day and night. He then left the city, and no one heard from him again. Another story says that Kintoki died at the age of fifty-five from a serious fever.

In Modern Stories

Kintarō and his likeness are still prevalent today. He is the inspiration for Sakata Gintoki in the manga and anime *Gintama*, although the author chose to use silver, *gin*, instead of gold, *kin*. In the 2001 Studio Ghibli movie *Spirited Away*, Yubaba's giant baby is wearing a Kintarō bib. His, though, has the character *bō* (坊), which means "boy," instead of Kintarō's *kin* (金). The manga *YuYu Hakusho* has a villainous version of the hero called Makintarō (魔金太郎)—literally "Evil Kintarō." Then lastly, in the game *Animal Crossing: New Leaf*, you can find a wig that resembles Kintarō's own hairstyle in the clothing shop Able Sisters.

KITSUNE

狐

Pronunciation: KEY-tsoo-nay

Translation: Foxes

Also known as: Bake Kitsune (化け狐), changing fox;
Yako (野狐), field fox; Yōko (妖狐), bewitching or calamitous fox;
Kyūbi no Kitsune (九尾の狐), nine-tailed fox

Overview

Kitsune are foxes that have been an integral part of Japanese culture since ancient times. They have turned up in historical texts, folklore, art, Noh plays, religious stories, superstitions, and have even been blamed for bodily and mental possessions. Kitsune are respected, worshipped, and feared. No matter how you look at it, these gorgeous, clever magical creatures just can't be ignored. Part of their irresistible appeal might be their extraordinary depth and multifaceted characters. They are at times contradictory, but they are always fascinating.

In Japan, two natural fox species exist: the Hokkaido fox and the Japanese red fox. However, when it comes to the more mystical and supernatural creatures—referred to as bake kitsune—the variations in characteristics are quite diverse. For example, bake kitsune can appear as a seductive shape-shifting beauty who drains men of their life essence, or it can be a doting mother and devoted wife. They can also be malicious spirits that possess people or bring ruin to entire family lines, or they can be messengers for the gods.

These latter type of kitsune are not just divine emissaries; sometimes, they are mistakenly revered as gods themselves. The god the fox serves is called Inari Ōkami (稲荷大神). People, recognizing the special connection between the two, offer prayers to the kitsune to pass on to Inari. They might ask for aid in a great number of areas, including: agriculture, fertility, fishing, business, sword making, clothing, shelter, family safety, tea, sake, prosperity, warfare, sex work, and more. Inari Shinkō (稲荷信仰) is a fox god faith—it's not quite a religion, but the fox is venerated. It is similar to Ōkami Shinkō (狼信仰), or wolf god faith (mentioned in the Ōkami entry) and Ryūjin Shinkō (龍神信仰), or dragon god faith (mentioned in the Ryū entry).

Background and Popular Stories

The fascination with foxes in Japanese culture may have started back in the Yayoi era (300 B.C.E.–C.E. 300), when rice farmers valued these crafty canines because they safeguarded their crops from rats and other rodents that would otherwise damage their harvests and undermine their fields. There was a touch of enchantment in the way foxes always appeared in spring, just as planting season arrived, offering their help in keeping varmints away. Shrines were even built to properly thank these hardworking animals.

It's very possible this long association with farming—especially rice—is what linked foxes to Inari Ōkami, also called Ōinari-san or Inari-sama, who is the goddess, god, or non-binary Shinto deity (it is sometimes said to be a combination of three to five different gods) that oversees agriculture. More than thirty thousand of the roughly eighty thousand shrines in Japan are Inari shrines. Many Inari shrines have a pair of fox statues on plinths stationed out front. Occasionally, you'll notice these venerable vulpines holding one of four items in their mouths or under their paws: rice

stalks (symbolizing abundant crops), a scroll (representing knowledge and wisdom and secret Inari techniques), a jewel, or a key (the jewel and key are held by pairs of foxes, with one fox holding each). The latter two items allude to the extremely elusive Jewel and Key Faith (玉鍵信仰), which is an obscure doctrine that involves the worship of Inari. In this belief system, the jewel represents the spiritual virtue of the Inari deity, and the key represents the desire to possess that virtue.

One distinctive trait about certain kitsune is that they grow more tails and become stronger as they age. The pinnacle of the kitsune hierarchy is the nine-tailed fox. Another characteristic is that kitsune are renowned for their remarkable shape-shifting abilities. Both male and female foxes can transform, and while the common perception is that they only turn into alluring women, they can take on a man's guise as well.

If you suspect a shape-shifting kitsune is masquerading as a human, offer it a drink of alcohol and keep an eye out for the moment it lets its guard down and its tail suddenly appears. Dogs are also adept at sniffing out a fox's true identity. Kitsune tend to avoid dogs for this very reason.

There is a famous tale called "The Legend of Tamamo no Mae," which recounts the story of the most powerful kitsune in history. There are different theories about Tamamo no Mae. Some people believe that she was a nine-tailed fox spirit that possessed various women throughout history (in China, India, and Japan), hopping from one body to the next over the centuries and causing pandemonium, disease, and destruction. (An interesting side note: Not so long ago, any kind of mental illness or odd behavior was thought to be brought about by possession by a fox spirit called kitsunetsuki (狐憑き).) The second theory of the legend suggests that it wasn't a fox spirit but a *real* fox that shape-shifted to become these strong women and courtesans through time. Since more instances call Tamamo no Mae a fox spirit, I'll refer to her as such here. There are some variations to the story, but the basic narrative is as follows.

Once upon a time, a powerful fox spirit possessed courtesans in both China and India, then finally, during the Heian era (C.E. 794–1185), arrived for the first time on Japanese soil in the form of Tamamo no Mae. Tamamo no Mae wasn't just extremely beautiful, she was also extremely intelligent. It was said there was no question she could not answer. She was also the favorite courtesan of Emperor Toba (1103–1156).

One day, out of the blue, the emperor fell deathly ill, and his mother blamed Tamamo no Mae. She called in an onmyōji (a powerful mystic) named Abe no Yasuchika (one of the famed Abe line—see the Abe no Seimei entry). He came to the conclusion that Tamamo no Mae was possessed by a wicked nine-tailed fox spirit, and he chased her from the household.

At this point, stories differ. Certain accounts describe Tamamo no Mae transforming herself into a sizable stone, while others say she hid inside the stone as a kitsune spirit. Alternatively, one version says she was killed, and the arrow used to hunt her down was a holy "Whistling Arrow." This specially carved arrow was believed to possess the ability to confine the nine-tailed fox's malevolent spirit within the rock for all time.

Still another legend says an army shot her with regular arrows, piercing her neck and flank, then a warrior arrived to finish her off with his sword. It was while dying or after her death that she changed into the stone, becoming trapped.

However it came about, whether due to the fox spirit or the fox itself, an association was forged with a large rock called the Sessho-seki (殺生石), translated as the "Life-Taking" or "Killing Stone." This stone is still located in a park north of Tokyo. Legend had it that any person or any animal that ventured too close to the stone ended up dead. But at least she was imprisoned there.

Then the unthinkable happened. On March 5, 2022, the Sessho-seki was discovered cracked in half. This caused quite a commotion in Japan and all over the world. Is this wicked nation-destroying kitsune again on the loose? On December 7, 2022, the carcasses of eight wild boars were found near the stone. Dead bodies of tanuki (Japanese raccoon dogs) and foxes had been found near the Sessho-seki before, but this was the first time something as large as a wild boar had been discovered.

In Modern Stories

There is no end to all the places the kitsune appears in manga, anime, games, and more. But here are a few especially popular ones: A nine-tailed fox spirit appears in the manga and anime *Naruto*. The manga and anime *Gingitsune: Messenger Fox of the Gods* is about a silver kitsune. And the manga *The Helpful Fox Senko-san* is about a cute young girl with fox ears who is actually an eight-hundred-year-old kitsune sent to help a businessman find happiness again.

NOW YOU KNOW

Kitsune love red azuki beans and abura-age (thin slices of tofu that have been deep-fried). Borrowing the name of the god, inari sushi is made with abura-age and is thus also a favorite of foxes. If you order kitsune udon or soba in Japan, you'll get a bowl of noodles with a couple of slices of abura-age on top.

KODAMA
木霊 or 木魂 or 木魅

Pronunciation: ko-DAH-mah

Translation: Tree Spirit

Etymology: There are three ways to write the word *kodama*.
The first character in all three means "tree," however the second one,
depending on which kanji you use, means "spirit" or "ghost," "soul," or
"fascination" or "charm."

Overview

A kodama is a mysterious tree spirit or kami (god) that's also considered a yōkai. It has several different manifestations or, oftentimes, no manifestation at all. Have you ever been deep in an old-growth forest and suddenly felt you weren't alone, as if a powerful and primeval presence was somewhere nearby, watching you? Well, you might not have been imagining it. This feeling very well could have been a kodama, or tree spirit.

Kodama are ancient phenomena in Japan, mentioned in both the *Kojiki* (a Japanese history text dating back to C.E. 712) and the *Nihon Shoki* (C.E. 720), where it was called a "tree god" or "spirit of the wood" and went by the name kukunochi no kami (久久能智神).

Kodama can surface as invisible presences, mysterious noises (such as sudden high screeching, groaning sounds, or unexplainable echoes), or—more rarely—various physical forms. One familiar manifestation of these tree spirits is a ghostly wisp or ball of light that floats through the trees. Other times it shows itself as an animal.

Background and Popular Stories

In some cases, a kodama can appear as a person, which happens if it feels the tree in which it resides is in danger of being cut down. The tree spirit will try desperately to communicate with the woodcutters and caution them not to fell the sacred tree (or trees).

One tactic it has at its disposal is to visit these workers in their dreams while disguised in human form. If the message in the dream is not received or it's ignored, the spirit may then turn wrathful and cause great misfortune and even death to those who refused to heed its warning. Conversely, properly worshipped and respected, the kodama can bring great fortune and good tidings to individuals as well as households, shrines, and entire villages. When you watch out for the trees, the trees watch out for you.

In addition to the earlier texts, kodama are also depicted in Toriyama Sekien's work *Gazu Hyakki Yagyō* (画図百鬼夜行), or *Illustrated Demon Horde's Night* Parade, from 1776. Sekien's piece shows an elderly man carrying a rake and an elderly woman holding a broom emerging from an old pine tree. He captioned the image: "When a tree reaches the age of one hundred years old, it gains a spirit that will allow itself to be seen."

While these old trees provide a place of residence for the kodama, the spirit itself is free to leave whenever it wants. It can go flitting about the woods, visiting other kodama, spooking unsuspecting hikers, or simply taking care of its main job, which is to protect the forest and make sure it stays healthy. Sometimes, though, if the mood strikes, it can transform into a human form and meet up with a strapping young logger.

In Modern Stories

Although kodama can appear in different forms—elderly gods, mysterious glowing spheres, animals, and humans—the image many people are probably most familiar with is from Miyazaki Hayao's 1997 film *Princess Mononoke*. Miyazaki created a very unique white ghostly version of the kodama that is both bizarre and enchantingly adorable. Then, of course, there are the Pokémon that are based on these tree spirits: Celebi, Phantump, and Trevenant.

KONAKI JIJI
子泣き爺

Pronunciation: KOH-nah-kee JEE-jee

Translation: Old Man Who Cries Like a Baby

Etymology: Ko (子) means "child," naki (泣き) means "to cry," and jiji (爺) means "old man."

Similar to: Ogyanaki (オギャナキ), Gogyanaki (ごギャナキ), Keshi Bōzu (芥子坊主), Poppy Boy(s)

Overview

The Konaki Jiji is a seemingly innocuous—but ultimately deadly—yōkai who hails from the southern island of Shikoku. His tale is simple and almost always the same: He kills someone who's just done a compassionate good deed. The target is out hiking alone when they hear crying. After a brief search, they find a child and pick it up. It's then they realize (too late) the thing they are holding is no ordinary baby—it's the Konaki Jiji. Unable to put it down, they are soon crushed by its increasing weight.

Two similar yōkai that are also found on Shikoku are the ogyanaki and gogyanaki. (In Japan, the onomatopoeia of a baby crying isn't "waah" but "ogya" or "gogya.") The two names might sound similar, but in fact, the creatures they describe are quite different. The ogyanaki cries but keeps itself invisible until the last minute. When it finally shows itself, it looks up at its victim and says, "Carry me!" The gogyanaki has an entirely different persona. It is a one-legged yōkai (see the Hitotsume Kozō entry for some other one-legged yōkai) that hops around aimlessly in the mountains crying, "Gogya! Gogya!" But you don't have to worry about it wanting to be picked up and turning you into a pile of human goo—its purpose is to predict earthquakes. Hearing and perhaps spotting a gogyanaki foretells a coming temblor.

There's one more rare yōkai that is somewhat related to the Konaki Jiji—the Keshi Bōzu. It's not one but rather a gang of baby yōkai that swarm up on you, crying shrilly. Once they have you cornered, they deftly shave off all your hair except the very top, leaving you completely bald save for a small patch of hair on top. You end up looking like a poppy flower after the petals have dropped. *Keshi Bōzu* means "Poppy Boy(s)" and was an actual hairstyle for small children back in the Edo era (1603–1867).

Background and Popular Stories

The classic tale of encountering the Konaki Jiji goes something like this. An innocent person is out walking on a path or in a field, a forest, or the mountains. Wherever they are, they're always alone—there is never anyone nearby to help when something goes awry.

At some point during their travels, they hear a baby crying. Their first thought is that it must be a child someone has abandoned. So, they hurry toward the sound, and sure enough, they see a baby just sitting there. They go over and scoop up the mewling babe and think, *Poor thing*. How lucky they just happened to be passing by.

But when they heft the little one up to get a good look at its face to make sure it's okay, they gasp.

Instead of a sweet, rosy-cheeked baby, they see the face of a wrinkled old man. That's when they realize their predicament: This isn't some neglected child. It's the Konaki Jiji! They know they're in trouble and need to get rid of the creature immediately, but when they try to set it back down, they find it's clinging to their clothes with enormous strength. They can't pull or pry it off. What's worse, it starts growing heavier and heavier. It increases in weight until the pitiful, kindhearted hiker is unable to stand up and falls to their knees. They know it is just a matter of time before they are completely crushed under the Konaki Jiji.

There is another series of similar folktales that also focus on the crying of a child but have a much bleaker history. They're based on the word *mabiki* (間引き), which means "to weed." If you plant a bunch of seeds and they all come up and start to crowd each other, you must sacrifice some of those seedlings so the others have room to grow.

The word *mabiki* and a macabre twist on its practice were prevalent during the Edo era (1603–1867). Drought, famine, disease, and disasters were common occurrences. When things were at their worst and parents had trouble feeding their families, sometimes mabiki was practiced on babies so that other children could survive.

The ghosts of these unfortunate babies—sacrificed so their siblings could have a better chance at living—have appeared all over Japan through the years, howling in the night and causing their own kind of creepy havoc.

In Modern Stories

Manga artist Mizuki Shigeru can be credited for gathering these obscure myths and folktales about the Konaki Jiji and introducing this sinister man baby into modern pop culture via his well-loved and long-running manga and anime *GeGeGe no Kitarō*.

In Mizuki Shigeru's depiction, however, the Konaki Jiji isn't the bad guy; he's part of the main character Kitarō's family. This Konaki Jiji helps protect Kitarō by clinging to enemies and turning to stone. Or, sometimes, he uses his cane or his head-butting skills to foil nasty opponents. He's also not a baby in Mizuki Shigeru's rendering but rather a little old man who claims to be 3,100 years old.

More recently, you'll find the little fighter in the game *Nioh 2*, and there, he's grown horns!

NOW YOU KNOW

If you've ever seen the Konaki Jiji in the manga or anime *GeGeGe no Kitarō*, you'll notice he's always wearing a straw old-fashioned rain cape and a bib or apron with the character *kin* (金), meaning "gold," "money," or "metal" on it. If this looks familiar, you're not imagining things. The folk hero Kintarō is often shown wearing the same garb. It's a symbol of strength and resilience. Judging by the 3,100-year-old Konaki Jiji's stamina and fighting ability, he's definitely earned the right to wear a similar outfit.

MOMOTARŌ

桃太郎

Pronunciation: MOH-moh-TAH-roh

Translation: The Peach Boy

Overview

Of the three big mythical folk heroes listed in this book—Kintarō, Urashima Tarō, and Momotarō—it is Momotarō who is the best known, both in Japan and abroad. Also known as the "Peach Boy," he's notorious for his bravery, strength, and kindheartedness.

In artwork, you'll see him depicted with his three animal friends: a monkey, a dog, and a pheasant. Any one of them might be carrying a banner flag that reads "Nihon Ichi (日本一)," or "Number One in Japan." Momotarō is usually dressed in fancy samurai attire with a white hachimaki headband tied around his head, and he carries a folding fan and a sword. Tied to his waist is a bag of kibidango, or millet dumplings (see sidebar at the end of this entry), which are popular in Okayama Prefecture.

Sometime in the 1930s, the idea came about that Okayama Prefecture was the birthplace of Momotarō. Much like how Kintarō is thought to be the real samurai Sakata no Kintoki as a child, someone suggested Momotarō might actually have been the hero Kibitsuhiko no Mikoto (吉備津彦命), the son of the seventh emperor (Emperor Kōrei), as a youth.

Since then, there has been a concerted effort to promote Okayama Prefecture as the birthplace of Momotarō. Although there are quite a few parallels, as you'll see in the following stories, some Momotarō enthusiasts refuse to believe the marketing campaigns.

Legend says that there was a brutal oni (ogre-like creature) named Ura (sometimes called Onra) who lived in a castle called Kinojō (鬼ノ城), literally Oni Castle. Ura brought suffering and chaos to everyone who lived near, yet no one was brave enough to try and oust him. It was only when the courageous Kibitsuhiko no Mikoto came along with three friends that the brutal ogre was finally conquered. After killing Ura, in order to avoid a curse the oni might place on them—even after its death—they put his head under a cauldron and buried it under the castle. Kinojō Castle's 1,300-year-old remains are still standing in Sōja City, Okayama Prefecture today.

Background and Popular Stories

Momotarō's story was passed down orally—changing naturally as it was told and retold—long before it was written down in the Edo era (1603–1867). A typical version you'll find in children's books goes like this.

Long ago, there was a kind old man and a kind old woman. They lived all alone in the hills, satisfied and happy with their simple life. At night, after an honest hard day's work, they would sit and reminisce about how good things were, except for one thing they truly missed: a child to love and dote on.

One day, following their normal routine, the old man trekked into the forest to cut wood while the old woman tottered over to the river to do laundry. But this day was different. As the old woman was scrubbing their clothes, she looked up to see a large peach floating down the rapids toward her. Shocked, she called to her husband, who came running, and together the two carried the peach into the house.

Excited about the unexpected treat, the old man lifted his axe to slice the peach in half, but just before he swung, out popped a small boy, who announced he had been sent by the gods to become their loving son. Elated, the couple named the boy Momotarō and loved and cherished him. Soon, though, they realized he wasn't like other children. Aside from being hatched from a giant fruit, he was incredibly strong. By the age of five, he was sawing down trees with dull knives.

When he was a little older, he announced that it was time for him to go to the wicked island of Onigashima (Ogre Island) and conquer the oni who terrorized the land and stole all the people's riches.

His parents were sad and worried but supported their son. His mother gave him a pouch filled with kibidango (millet dumplings), and together his aging parents sent him off. Along the way to Onigashima, Momotarō met and befriended three animals: a dog, a monkey, and a pheasant. He gave them some of his mother's kibidango in exchange for their help in battling the oni. The four reached the island, fought the oni, and won. They gathered and returned all the treasure that had been pilfered from the villagers throughout the years, then returned home heroes.

A much older—and much less child-friendly—version of the story doesn't have Momotarō springing from the peach. Instead, the elderly couple devour the peach, which causes them to get frisky—and fertile—again. Ten months later, the old woman gives birth to the boy, and they name him after that mysterious, magical aphrodisiac fruit.

In Modern Stories

In the early- to mid-1940s, Momotarō's adventure with his animal friends and their defeat of the oni probably felt like the perfect metaphor as Japan entered World War II. That could be why the naval ministry ordered animator, screenwriter, and director Mitsuyo Seo to put out two animated films featuring the popular hero in a much more contemporary dilemma. And that's how the beloved Momotarō got caught up and used in war propaganda.

The two films in question are the thirty-seven-minute-long *Momotaro's Sea Eagles* (1943) and its sequel, the seventy-four-minute *Momotaro: Sacred Sailors*, sometimes called *Momotaro's Divine Sea Warriors* (1945), which was also the first feature-length animated film in Japan. Both show Momotarō and his adorable animal buddies battling their enemy—not on the distant Onigashima but in much less fictional places: aboard a ship, in a Zero fighter, and on a much different island.

It's said the naval ministry showed Mitsuyo Seo Disney's *Fantasia* for inspiration, but he undoubtedly, somewhere along the line, also watched the then-popular-in-the-West cartoon *Popeye*. This is evident in the fact that the main adversary in *Momotaro: Sacred Sailors* (the American) was drawn as the spitting image of Bluto but with a single horn on his head à la an oni. Instead of popping a can of spinach, the cute animal pilots noshed on kibidango and flexed their muscles to show the miraculous effect.

Using the likeness of Momotarō for propaganda purposes wasn't new to World War II, though. In both the Sino-Japanese War (1894–1895) and the Russo-Japanese War (1904–1905), cartoonish images of the kindhearted Peach Boy preparing for battle were also used.

In even more modern times, Momotarō, like folk heroes Kintarō and Urashima Tarō, pops up often in games, manga, anime, and comics. There's the Nintendo Switch game *Momotaro Dentetsu* and the manga series *YuYu Hakusho*, where he's imagined as an anti-Momotarō known as Kuro Momotarō (Black Momotarō) or, in the English language version, Poison Peach Boy. There's also a Chicago-based Japanese restaurant that opened in 2014 called Momotaro, a Momotarō cocktail that comes complete with a splash of peach wine, and Momotaro Jeans, which have a logo featuring the Peach Boy wearing a pair of jeans and standing behind an oversized peach.

NOW YOU KNOW

Kibidango are a type of wagashi (和菓子), or a Japanese-style sweet, that hail from Okayama Prefecture. The kibidango you come across now aren't exactly the same ones the legendary Peach Boy and his animal friends enjoyed, though. Millet dumplings today contain little to no millet and are instead soft, lightly sweetened mochi balls. Regardless, they're still a delightful souvenir from Okayama.

NINGYO

人魚

Pronunciation: NEEN-gyoh

Translation: Human Fish, Mermaid

Etymology: The word is literally the characters for "human" and "fish."

Also known as: Teijin (低人)

Similar to: Hatsugyo (髪魚), Hair Fish; Jinjahime (神社姫), Shrine Princess; Himeuo (姫魚), Princess Fish; Ainusokki (アイヌソッキ), mermaid of the Ainu, Hokkaido's Indigenous people; and the prophetic yōkai

---

Overview

Japanese mermaids aren't the curvy, flaxen-haired, bronze-skinned, seashell-bikini-topped visions that they are in the West. As a matter of fact, they're kind of the opposite—they're scary looking. Ningyo mummies in museums or enshrined in temples across the country show them more closely resembling Fiji (or Feejee) mermaids, those grotesque little mummified creatures with razor-like teeth that appear to have died screaming and made the rounds in the Barnum & Bailey Circus back in the 1800s. In artwork and legends, however, there are quite a few variations. There is everything from beautiful armless creatures with perfect Japanese hairstyles; to red-bellied, horned, serpent-like creatures; to a cross between a fish and a child that bawls when you catch it.

An ancient story describes how 1,400 years ago, in Shiga Prefecture, Prince Shōtoku (C.E. 574–622) was strolling along the shore of Lake Biwa when a ningyo popped up and told him how, in a previous life, it had been a fisherman. As payback for all the sea creatures it took, it had been reborn as a mermaid. It pleaded with the prince to display its horrible mummified remains after it died as a reminder to others to not kill all the time, because life is precious. The water beast then died right there.

Prince Shōtoku scooped it up and granted the creature's last wish. Today, that same mummy is said to reside at the Tenshō Kyōsha Shrine (天照教本社) in Fujinomiya City.

Mermaids or human-fish combinations have an incredibly long and interesting history in Japan, sometimes bestowing good luck, sometimes bringing or predicting disaster. Sometimes they were released to avoid problems; other times they were killed out of fear. At least once, a mermaid was eaten.

Background and Popular Stories

Undoubtedly, the best-known mermaid story in Japan is the legend of Yaobikuni (八百比丘尼). Her name means "Eight-Hundred-Year-Old Nun," and her story goes something like this. Once upon a time, a man caught a very strange fish. He took it home and invited over all his friends and relatives to eat it with him. Everyone waited while he was preparing the meal. One guest was particularly eager to see what was so special about this fish. He peeked into the kitchen and saw that the animal being readied had a human face! He returned to the others and warned them, telling them not to eat it.

The fisherman brought out the meal all cut up on a platter, and everyone feigned joy as they plucked up pieces with their chopsticks and pretended to eat them, but they were really hiding the horrid meat in their clothes to dispose of later.

After the party, one of the members returned home very drunk. When he walked in, his daughter ran up to him excitedly, asking where her souvenir was. Without thinking, he pulled out the mermaid flesh and gave it to her. The little girl popped it into her mouth and swallowed.

Her father tried to stop her, but it was too late. He felt horrible and kept an eye on her, thinking she'd been poisoned, but nothing happened. The little girl grew up and got married.

But then things changed after that. Suddenly, she stopped aging. Everyone around her grew old and died, but she stayed young. She outlived her husband, married again, and again. She then decided to become a nun and lived the rest of her life traveling to various countries, until finally, at the age of eight hundred, she returned home and died.

In rare instances, humans have killed ningyo. For example, back in 1805 in Shinminato City, Toyama Prefecture, a ningyo emerged from the sea and threatened some fishermen. The men claimed they had to kill it to save their lives. It took a combined 450 guns to defeat the 36-foot-long (11-meter) golden-horned ningyo who had a red underbelly and a face that resembled a hannya (般若) mask, which has two sharp horns, metallic eyes, and a horrific expression that represents a jealous female demon in Noh theater. The sea monster's dying cries were reported to be heard up to 2.5 miles (4 kilometers) away. Posthumously, they called it Kairai (海雷), or Sea Thunder. After all the excitement died down, it was guessed that perhaps it might have been a jinja-hime (see the Amabie entry) sent by the dragon god, Ryūjin, who lives under the sea, and wanted to deliver an important message—only, now they'd never know.

Another aquatic yōkai that's similar but considered a kind of pre-ningyo because it's so old is the disturbingly named hair fish, or hatsugyo (髪魚). This is a fish with a face that is eerily humanlike, made all the more unsettling because it also has long hair on its head. Sometimes this creature cries like a baby when caught. One story of a hatsugyo comes from the reign of Empress Suiko (C.E. 592–628). It describes a suspicious fish that appeared in the Gamō River in Ōmi (now Shiga Prefecture). It was described as looking like a cross between a child and a fish.

Another hatsugyo tale tells of a man who was fishing in a large pond and caught a fish with shining white scales and hair on its head. He brought it home and put it in a tub, covering it with a lid. That night, though, he had a vivid dream in which the self-proclaimed "god of fish" appeared and scolded him, saying, "Why did you imprison my relative?" The next morning when he went to check on his strange human-haired fish, it was gone. In more recent times, it's believed this mysterious aquatic critter might have been a rarely seen oarfish, which is shiny and has long hairlike strands on its head.

In Modern Stories

The Studio Ghibli film *Ponyo* (2008) is about a cute little human-faced fish. Yaobikuni appears as a gorgeous creature in the game *Onmyoji*, in the manga *Air*, and as an old nun in *Blade of the Immortal*. Also, the manga and anime series *Mermaid Saga* is all about ningyo.

NOPPERABŌ

のっぺらぼう

Pronunciation: NOH-peh-rah-BOH

Etymology: The word *nopperi* (のっぺり) describes the state of being flat or spread out. *Bō* (坊) is an affectionate suffix attached to boys' names.

Similar to: Nuppeppō (ぬっぺっぽう)

Overview

The nopperabō is another harmless yōkai, but you'd never know that by looking at it. Its main purpose is to startle unfortunate passersby using its most unsettling yet simple appearance: It has a human form but no face. Where there should be eyes, a nose, and a mouth is perfectly smooth skin.

Stories about the nopperabō range from the annoying to the scary. Sometimes it just shows up as is out of nowhere to frighten you, but it is also capable of appearing as if it has a face, only to—once it gets your attention—reach up and dramatically wipe that same face off. Whatever the technique, there are many tales of innocent people encountering this perplexing yōkai.

Like many yōkai, the nature and origins of the nopperabō have different interpretations. When it comes to this yōkai, there are two main schools of thought:

1. In the first, the nopperabō is a distinct yōkai with its own unique characteristics. Its only disguise is to temporarily pretend to be human so that when it reveals its true nature, it gets maximum shock value.
2. In the second, the nopperabō is some other shape-shifting entity, specifically a tanuki (Japanese raccoon dog), a fox, or a mujina (an old term that can refer to a tanuki, badger, or masked palm civet). These creatures are all believed to have the ability to transform into humans and then change their faces to be featureless.

The latter interpretation seems supported by a story in *Shinsetsu Hyakumonogatari,* a 1767 collection of ghost stories. That book describes someone who was surprised by a nopperabō on a bridge and then later discovered some thick hairs on their clothing. This led to the conclusion the no-faced monster must certainly be a fox, tanuki, or mujina in disguise.

If the nopperabō is in fact simply a mujina in disguise, then it was mentioned all the way back in the *Nihon Shoki* (C.E. 720). According to that text, during spring, mujina would appear and shape-shift into humans and sing songs.

Background and Popular Stories

While there are numerous accounts of run-ins with this faceless creeper, probably the best known was written by the master writer and translator Lafcadio Hearn. His short story entitled "Mujina" (found in his 1904 book *Kwaidan: Stories and Studies of Strange Things*) goes something like this:

Once, on the Akasaka Road in Tokyo, there was a place called the Slope of the Province of Kii. On one side of the road was an ancient moat, and on the other were high stone walls of an imperial palace. This was back before the era of streetlamps, and the roads were very dark after nightfall. Once the

sun had set, pedestrians would go miles out of their way to avoid this particular slope. It was said that mujina had been spotted there.

One night, a man was out walking along the sloping road when he saw a young woman crouched by the moat, weeping. He was concerned she might throw herself into the water, so he called out to her.

"Please do not cry. If there is any way I can, I shall be glad to help."

But the woman continued hiding her face under one of her long sleeves, sobbing. The man moved closer.

"Please, don't cry."

The woman stood up, her back to him, her face still concealed. When he was right behind her, he reached over and lightly touched her shoulder.

"Listen to me...."

The young woman then turned, dropped her arm, reached up, and stroked her completely smooth face with her hand.

The man screamed and ran away. He fled up the Slope of the Province of Kii and ran into that black darkness. But he dared not look back—there was no telling what was following him. Finally, up ahead he saw a small light. As he got closer, he recognized it was the lantern of a traveling soba seller.

The man felt immediate relief at having found human companionship again. He fell down at the feet of the soba seller and cried out.

"What happened? Did someone hurt you? Was it robbers?" the soba seller asked.

"Not robbers," gasped the man. "I saw a woman by the moat, and she showed me—ah! I cannot tell you what she showed me."

"Was it anything like this?" the soba seller said, reaching up and stroking his hand down his face, turning it into the smoothness of an egg. At that moment, the lantern light went out.

In Modern Stories

The nopperabō's influence can be found in several other places nowadays. The creepypasta Internet meme and urban legend Slenderman are depicted as having nothing but a smooth face, as are the nurses in the horror game *Silent Hill 2*. Another interesting possible influence of the nopperabō is the character Koh in *Avatar: the Last Airbender*.

The most traditional nopperabō in modern times, though, is found in the Studio Ghibli movie *Pom Poko* (1994), where a more modern version of Lafcadio Hearn's story "Mujina" is shown. In this version, a young police officer tries to console a crying young woman...and we know what happens next!

NOW YOU KNOW

The nuppeppō is sometimes confused with the nopperabō. There are some major differences, though. The nuppeppō creeps around abandoned temples and graveyards at night, walking aimlessly on its tiny legs. The creature's body is a huge blob with wrinkles and folds, creating the illusion that it's just one big face. Additional folds give the impression of little arms. The nuppeppō does have a similar purpose to the nopperabō: to frighten you. Which is sure to happen once you realize it's made entirely of decaying flesh.

NUE

鵺 or 鵼

Pronunciation: NOO-eh

Etymology: Both characters for the nue are composed
of two parts. One kanji is a combination of parts meaning
"sky" and "bird," and the other is made up of "night" and "bird."

Overview

The nue is a wingless flying beast comprised of various animal parts. It is both a harbinger and bringer of suffering, calamity, and political unrest. Even those who only hear its eerie cry (*Hyoo! Hyoo!*) are said to fall upon misfortune. It is considered one of the more elusive yōkai, despite the fact that there have been many sightings of this dangerous chimera.

A notable account of the nue can be found in *Heike Monogatari* (平家物語), or *The Tale of Heike*, a collection of oral stories recited by traveling monks. The most popular versions were put together by a blind monk named Kakuichi in 1371.

In this compilation, the nue is said to have the face of a monkey, the body of a tanuki (Japanese raccoon dog), the limbs of a tiger, and the tail of a snake. Some variations have the tiger legs and tanuki body switched, so the body is striped and the limbs resemble those of a tanuki. At least one documented description from the Muromachi era (1336–1573) suggests a significantly less imposing appearance, where the nue is made up of the head of a cat and the body of a chicken.

If you look closely, you'll notice something that stands out as odd about the nue (other than its overall appearance, that is). Despite it being referred to as a flying creature with the character for bird in its name, the nue lacks wings. Indeed, no one knows how or why it can fly. It just does.

While descriptions of the nue say it has the tail *of* a snake, you'll often see it depicted with a snake *as a tail*. The end of the snake tail is the actual snake's head, which angrily flicks out its tongue or spits fire.

Background and Popular Stories

The following is a retelling of a popular nue legend: Once upon a time, in the year 1153, night after night, a bank of black clouds emerged, covering the sky above the imperial palace. When they did, a pall fell over the entire city. Even the emperor at the time, Emperor Konoe, was affected by this strange phenomenon, suffering relentless nightmares and growing weaker and weaker by the night.

At a loss for what to do, all the emperor's courtiers gathered to discuss the situation and agreed that it must be a nue. However, because the nue always remained hidden above the black clouds, it was impossible to defeat. Even the monks who sent up prayers to disperse it had no luck.

They finally decided to call upon the renowned samurai and famed archer Minamoto no Yorimasa to quell the horrid sky beast. After visiting a shrine (now known as the Yorimasa Shrine), he and his loyal follower, Ino Hayata, set out at the hour of the ox (2 a.m.)—the same time the nue arrived concealed in a mass of roiling clouds every night.

Minamoto no Yorimasa scanned the sky with his keen eyes and spotted the outline of the giant monster. He recited a quick mantra, a kind of Buddhist chant or prayer, then used his ancestral bow, named Raishōōdō or

Raijōdō (雷上動), which means "Moving above Thunder," and shot a single arrow at the ominous black cloud bank. He struck his target precisely.

Bellowing a bloodcurdling cry, the nue plummeted to the earth and landed near the northern part of Nijo Castle. Ino Hayata ran over and finished it off with his sword. The vanquished nue was then paraded throughout the city to celebrate the end of the wretched days and reassure everyone that it was indeed dead.

After the nue was slain, Yorimasa was presented with a tachi sword (an older style sword, the predecessor to the katana) named Shishiō (獅子王), loosely translated as "Lion King" or "King of Lions." This sword can be viewed today in the Tokyo National Museum in Taito Ward, Tokyo.

One alternate ending to the story says that after striking down the vexing nue, two or three cries of a cuckoo bird were heard, and peace returned to the land. The emperor regained his health too.

Yet another ending tells that after the people so gloatingly celebrated the creature's demise, an epidemic swept through the town, killing many—perhaps from a curse. Realizing that, even in death, the monster was making trouble and something needed to be done, they hauled its corpse into a canoe and floated it down the river.

Here the story fragments again. One legend says the nue was buried at the famous Kiyomizu Temple. In another more interesting ending, the canoe washed ashore in Higashinari Ward in Osaka. The villagers and priests, rightfully shaken by the giant dead hodgepodge of a monster, did the right thing and gave it a proper funeral ceremony, buried it, and built a mound to honor it. The grave was honored for hundreds of years, until sometime in the Meiji era (1868–1912), when it was destroyed to make room for construction. Almost immediately, the angry spirit of the nue began tormenting those who lived nearby, the development project was stopped, and the small burial mound paying tribute to the nue was rebuilt. It is still in existence today. Sadly, though, it's not in the exact location as before. It has been moved and repaired due to being burned during World War II. You can still see the burn marks on the stone. It's believed that praying at this grave, called the Nue Zuka (鵺塚), will bring about healing of childhood diseases.

In Modern Stories

The nue makes its fearsome appearance in numerous anime, manga, and games. It shows up as Zabimaru in *Bleach* and appears unnamed in *Nioh 2*, *Boruto: Naruto Next Generations*, and *Dororo*. The nue turns up as a boss character in the video game *Persona 5*, complete with a snake with glowing yellow eyes for a tail. Its face isn't a monkey, though, but all black with a thick white mane. More traditionally, the dangerous monster is featured in the Noh play "Nue," written by Zeami Motokiyo.

NOW YOU KNOW

The nue is known for its mournful cry, and there really is a nocturnal bird called a toratsugumi, nicknamed the "nue." In English, it's called a White's thrush. It makes a long, forlorn whistling sound like *Hyoo! Hyoo!*

ŌKAMI

狼

Pronunciation: OH-kah-mee

Translation: Wolf

Also known as: Yamainu (山犬), Oinu-sama (お犬様),
Okuriinu (送り犬), Mukaeinu (迎え犬)

Overview

The ōkami (wolf) is the lesser known of the canine yōkai. Similar to its wildly popular cousin the kitsune, there were two species of Japanese wolf that actually existed—the Hokkaido and the Honshu. Sadly, the Hokkaido wolf became extinct in 1889 and the Honshu wolf in 1905. Maybe that's why you don't hear about this animal or its majestic yōkai version nearly as much as you do the fox. But that doesn't mean it wasn't extremely important throughout Japanese history. Both the kitsune and the ōkami commanded respect and fear. According to some, the fox is the messenger of the rice field gods (Inari) and the wolf was the messenger of the mountain gods.

In ancient times, wolves were regarded as guardians because they preyed on boars, deer, and monkeys, which were known to ravage and destroy crops. The wolves' appetites were sated by these animals, so they rarely attacked humans. This symbiotic relationship lasted for centuries. Until after World War II when Americans introduced strychnine.

There was a related yōkai called the okuriinu (送り犬), meaning "escorting dog" or "sending-off dog." In old Japan, the word *inu* (dog) was often used as a synonym for both wolf and fox (you'll read more about this topic soon as it relates to inugami, meaning "dog god"). These stoic beasts lived in the mountains and watched over travelers, protecting them and guiding them home. Well, unless they collapsed from exhaustion—then they'd get eaten right up. If, though, the wayfarers were only resting, the okuriinu would keep its distance and continue to safeguard their journey. It was still an uneasy experience.

Once the traveler made it home safely, it was custom to turn, bow, say goodbye to the escorting wolf, and thank it properly, maybe by giving it some food or a single tabi straw sandal. After this, the animal would mysteriously disappear back into the forest.

Background and Popular Stories

There are still hundreds of wolf shrines in existence all over Japan. Out of all of them, two are central to wolf lore: the Mitsumine Shrine (三峯神社) founded around 2,000 years ago and located in the mountains of Chichibu, Saitama Prefecture and the Musashi Mitake Shrine (武蔵御嶽神社) on Mount Mitake founded more than 1,200 years ago by Prince Yamato Takeru no Mikoto (Yamato Takeru for short).

The latter shrine's story goes something like this: Yamato Takeru, the legendary unifier of Japan and the son of the twelfth emperor, was traveling on a military expedition when an evil spirit in the form of a stag appeared, bringing with it a thick mist. The animal then proceeded to lead Yamato Takeru and his group astray. Before they knew it, they were hopelessly lost deep in the mountains. When they looked around, the stag had vanished. Unsure which way to go or what to do, they decided to stop moving altogether. Unexpectedly, just when all was at its bleakest, a white wolf—a god in disguise—appeared to guide them out of the mountains. Yamato Takeru

was so grateful and moved by this divine animal's actions that he told it to remain there on the mountain, fight off evil, and become the Ōguchi no Makami (大口の真神), or True God with the Big Mouth.

A series of folk stories written by the author Koyama Masao was published in the Showa era (1926–1989). One of the tales is about one of these okuriinu, escorting dogs.

Once upon a time, there was a very pregnant woman who was returning to her parents' home to give birth (as is custom, even now). Unfortunately, on the way home, while traversing hills alone, she went into labor. Night fell, and she delivered the baby there on a mountain path. Soon, many wolves gathered around her and the newborn babe.

Exhausted and hopeless, the distraught woman cried out, "If you're going to eat us, then just eat us!"

But instead, the animals spent the entire night protecting the mother and child from all the other wicked things that lurked in the forest.

The next day, her strength renewed, and she and her baby were able to make it to her parents' house.

Later, after hearing this story, her husband went to thank these okuriinu for watching over his wife and child. He presented them with sekihan, red beans mixed with mochi rice, the quintessential celebratory dish usually served only on festive and auspicious occasions.

There are a couple more wolf legends as well. One is about wolves raising a baby that was left in the forest. Afterward, that same child grew up to become the leader Fujiwara no Hidehira.

Wolves are also said to have howled before a flood in 1889, thus warning the villagers near Mount Tamaki of the danger. Later, the wolves got a tree named after them for this act of kindness. It's called the Cypress of the Dog Howls.

Another old wives' tale is that sometimes if a family member did not return home from a long journey in the mountains, a wolf would appear at the person's home and howl sadly, letting their family know that they had died.

As stories about wolves and dogs sometimes overlapped, it's worth mentioning that there was a brutal ritual called inugami (犬神 or 狗神), which means "dog god" or "dog spirit." Inugami was a powerful curse that employed a dog's spirit in order to torment one's enemies. It involved truly awful methods of torturing and killing an animal in the belief that its enraged spirit would return to harm a targeted individual. According to folktales, certain types of people—those with unstable emotions, for example—could attract an inugami unknowingly. If not removed properly, the inugami could inhabit entire bloodlines, and there were families who were thought to be possessed for generations. This is similar to kitsunetsuki, or fox possession (see the Kitsune entry). In parts of the southern island of Shikoku, there was even an old custom to make sure one wasn't marrying into an inugami family before they tied the knot. The method of applying the curse was banned in the Heian era.

Similar to the Ryūjin Shinkō (龍神信仰), or dragon god faith (see the Ryū entry), and the Inari Shinkō (稲荷信仰), or fox god faith (see the Kitsune entry), there was an Ōkami Shinkō (狼信仰), or wolf god faith, in which wolves were venerated.

In Modern Stories

Moro no Kimi in Studio Ghibli's *Princess Mononoke* (1997) is a three-hundred-year-old white wolf who raised the main character, San, from a baby. The video game *Ōkami* features another depiction of a wolf—Amaterasu. The game, though, uses the kanji "big god" (大神) which is a homophone for wolf. But also the Japanese mythical sun goddess Amaterasu is indeed a "big god" and here she takes the form of a white wolf. Inugami also appear in the manga and anime *Yo-kai Watch*, *Gintama*, and *Inuyasha*.

ONI

鬼

Pronunciation: OH-nee

Translation: Ogre or Demon

Similar to: Kijo (鬼女), Yamauba (山姥),
also pronounced Yamanba; both female oni

Overview

Oni is often translated as "ogre" or "demon," but those monikers don't do justice to these complex Japanese beasts. The basic oni as they appear these days are ogre-like monsters many times larger than humans, heavily muscled, with skin tones of red or blue (or sometimes green). They have two horns on their heads, extremely fierce expressions on their faces, and sharp fangs. Naked from the waist up, they're usually seen wearing tiger-skin loincloths and iron rings around their ankles and wrists. They carry studded iron clubs. Not that they need them—oni are unbelievably strong, voracious, bloodthirsty, and, except for a few outliers, downright evil.

Oni of old, though, were actually more diverse. They appeared in a greater variety of colors (black, white, yellow, multicolored) and had any number of eyes, from one to dozens, and there were even some that were one-legged. Then there were oni that were more or less invisible wicked entities up to no good.

Oni were originally from China but have taken on a life of their own in Japan, evolving through the ages. There are several lineages of oni that are still debated by scholars and folklorists. One obvious origin story can be found in the mythical beginnings of Japan. A kind of pre-oni race called the yomotsushikome (黄泉醜女), which means "fearful creatures of the underworld," was mentioned in the *Kojiki* (C.E. 712) as a band of terrible ogre-like monsters sent to avenge the divine female creator of Japan, Izanami. (You can find more on her story in the Raijin and Fūjin entry.)

A second genesis of the Japanese oni myth is Buddhism. Buddhist hells are especially grotesque and ghastly. If you're ever unfortunate enough to find yourself in one, you'll first be met by Gozu (牛頭) and Mezu (馬頭), which are a cow-head oni and a horse-head oni. Once inside, a plethora of other heinous oni will be waiting to skewer you with long blades, pour boiling iron all over you, or stir you into a pot of pus and blood for the rest of eternity.

Then there's also the esoteric practice of Onmyōdō, where powerful onmyōji (mystical diviners) can conjure and control shikigami (式神), which are also called kijin (鬼神), whose characters mean "oni" and "god." Onmyōji are rumored to create these demon beasts, too, and manipulate them as needed.

Background and Popular Stories

One of the most famous folktales about an oni is the story of Shuten Dōji (酒呑童子), whose name means "Sake Drinking Lad." But Shuten Dōji was no innocent lad—he was 50 feet (15 meters) tall and by some accounts had a crimson-colored body, five horns on his head, and fifteen eyes. Rumor had it that Shuten Dōji's father was Yamata no Orochi, the eight-headed dragon. Shuten Dōji was and still is considered the strongest and most loathsome oni in Japan's history. His tale goes something like this.

Once upon a time, back when Japan's capital was Kyoto, women and young girls started disappearing from the streets and even their own homes. The famed onmyōji Abe no Seimei was consulted, and it was determined that the culprit was a heinous oni named Shuten Dōji and his group of lesser ogre who lived up on Mount Oe. This savage gang were notorious for getting drunk, kidnapping young women, and both drinking their blood and eating their flesh. The legendary Minamoto no Yorimitsu (源頼光) (C.E. 948–1021) was called, along with his Shitennō (四天王), or Four Heavenly Kings, the famous band of samurai Yorimitsu always fought with (one of them being Sakata no Kintoki—see the Kintarō entry). Disguised as monks, the five samurai hid their weapons inside their billowy robes and prepared to defeat the monster.

After praying at a couple of shrines, the warriors set out. Still not exactly sure what their plan was and deep in the mountains, they were met by several old men (who were actually gods in disguise). The elderly deities presented the men with a jug of magical sake and some advice. If Shuten Dōji—who drank constantly but never lost consciousness—were to consume this divine drink, he would, in fact, pass out. The rest was up to them.

Later that night, gathered around the abominable feasting table, Minamoto no Yorimitsu secretly served the charmed sake to Shuten Dōji and it worked. Once the giant was asleep, Minamoto no Yorimitsu chopped off his head. But instead of falling to the floor, the enormous head flew at Yorimitsu, gnashing its teeth. It latched on to the warrior's helmet and bit down. Luckily, the great samurai just happened to be wearing two helmets that day. Eventually, the five samurai defeated the beast and his minions and rescued all the kidnapped—not yet eaten—young women and took them home.

Another interesting superstition about the oni involves the northeastern sections of homes, buildings, and even cities. This area is called the kimon (鬼門), or demon's gate, and it is believed to be very unlucky. The belief system of Onmyōdō posits that it is here yin energy changes into yang energy, thus making it unstable and chaotic. Other theories hold that it's the direction from which the coldest winds in the winter blow or that it's where spirits pass through. Whatever the reason, the kimon is the place where oni come into your home, steal all your good luck, and unleash adversity.

The topic is quite complicated, and there are more than a few differing belief systems, but as a general rule, when building a house, you should never put a window, door, or anything related to water (such as a toilet) or fire (such as a stove) in the northeast part of the house. Windows and doors make it easier for the oni to enter, and fire and water rile up the demons, making them more dangerous. In Japan, contractors are aware of this superstition and will help design your home accordingly. If all else fails, a well-placed ofuda (お札) (talisman) or a monkey or blue dragon figurine might help ward off the misfortune-bringing ogres.

In older times, entire cities were planned in order to protect this vulnerable sector. Kyoto's Enrakuji complex on Mount Hiei was built on the kimon of the city in hopes that the positive power of the temples would dispel any oni with malicious intent. If you walk around the Kyoto Imperial Palace, you'll notice it is notched—the northeast corner actually has an indentation that symbolically erases the dangerous gateway for bad luck.

Other ways to help protect yourself from oni include keeping your kimon clean and placing some lucky items there, or planting a prickly holly bush in your yard (oni dislike thorny leaves).

February 3 in Japan is Setsubun (節分), or Bean-Throwing Day, marking the transition from winter to spring. On this day, families all across Japan throw handfuls of roasted soybeans outside, yelling, "Oni wa soto!" (Oni, outside!), and then toss more beans inside with the call, "Fuku wa uchi!" (Good luck, inside!). Sometimes people will dress up as oni on this day and children will pelt them with soybeans. Also, on Setsubun, people eat the same number of soybeans as their age to ensure good luck and health in the coming year.

In Modern Stories

Despite their nastiness, Oni are everywhere in popular culture. Some places you might have seen them are the manga and anime *Inuyasha* and *Demon Slayer* and the Netflix show *Oni: Thunder God's Tale*. Although the show is called *Oni: Thunder God's Tale*, the main character Naridon is actually Raijin (see the entry on Raijin and Fūjin).

ONIBI AND KITSUNEBI

鬼火 and 狐火

Pronunciation: OH-nee-bee and KEY-tsoo-nay-bee

Translation: Demon Fires and Fox Fires

Onibi are also known as: Chōchinbi (提灯火),
lantern fire; Tenbi (天火), heaven fires; as well as various
other regional names

Kitsunebi are also known as: Hitobosu or Hitomoshi (火点し),
fire lighting; Rinka (燐火), phosphorus fire; these occurrences, too,
have many varying local names

Overview

The onibi and the kitsunebi are similar—but ultimately different—otherworldly phenomena that appear as ghostly lights in the night sky. They can manifest as a single ethereal blue candlelight floating in a graveyard on a hot summer night, or a winding procession of red and orange paper-lantern-looking lights, flickering on a hillside where no roads or people are known to exist.

When talking about these mysterious ghostly illuminations, confusion and overlap reign supreme, at times even confounding folklorists and scholars. This is mostly due to local disparities and differing stories through time. Keeping that in mind, there are two names that stand out: The onibi (demon fires) and kitsunebi (fox fires). Let's see if we can learn the distinctions between the two.

Background and Popular Stories

Here's what we know about kitsunebi: They were depicted in Utagawa Hiroshige's (1797–1858) woodblock print *New Year's Eve Foxfires at the Changing Tree*. The image is of a legend that says on the last day of every year, foxes from all over the Kantō area (which consists of seven prefectures: Gunma, Tochigi, Ibaraki, Saitama, Tokyo, Chiba, and Kanagawa) headed to Ōji Inari Shrine (王子稲荷神社) in Tokyo. On the way, they always stopped under the same large enoki (hackberry) tree to change into their formal attire before continuing on to the shrine, where they would pay their respects to the head Inari god (for more on Inari, see the Kitsune entry). This nocturnal parade of foxes was a spectacular sight, even when viewed from afar. What made it truly captivating was that all the animals in attendance exhaled small balls of fire that burned sublimely in front of their mouths. Observant farmers used to watch and count these kitsunebi, using the number as an indicator to forecast the prosperity of the upcoming year's harvests. The higher the number, the better the harvest.

There are a couple of other theories about how foxes became able to produce these ghostly glowing wisps. One is that foxes of yore could only shape-shift into people under certain circumstances. Once a kitsune had reached the age of either fifty or one hundred (different stories give different ages), they could place a human skull on their head and bow to the Big Dipper. If they managed this without the skull falling off, they were then able to transform. A related belief suggests they did this ritual with a human bone clenched in their teeth and that the bone emitted that spectral light called a kitsunebi.

A second sillier theory is that kitsune caused the ghostly flames by smacking their tails against the ground. This long association between foxes and fire led naturally to the suspicion that foxes started real fires (see the following story).

Onibi, or demon fires, are somewhat different. These, too, are eerie lights at night, but they derive from the corpses of both people and animals. The light is usually blue, but red or orange (like a kitsunebi) is sometimes reported. One of the oldest mentions of the onibi is recorded in the *Wakan Sansai Zue* (和漢三才図会), or *Illustrated Sino-Japanese Encyclopedia* (1712). This book states that if someone ran across several of these blue lights floating 3–6 feet (1–2 meters) above the ground, they would have their soul sucked out.

Onibi tend to prefer marshy land, forests, and graveyards. Because of the latter, there's the opinion that the onibi lights have nothing to do with fire at all but are created from the trace amounts of phosphorus (or perhaps phosphine or hydrogen sulfide) that is produced from decaying corpses. The fact that they seem to move around is just an optical illusion.

Onibi include so many types of luminescent orbs, the term itself has been used to collectively refer to kitsunebi, hitodama (see the sidebar), and other will-o'-the-wisps.

There are folktales that illustrate the myth that foxes start fires. Consider, for example, the story of a samurai who served a provincial governor of Kai Province (present-day Yamanashi Prefecture). One evening, this samurai left the governor's office, got on his horse, and headed home like he always did. Only this time, when he was about halfway there, he encountered a fox.

The samurai chased the animal down, drew his bow, and shot it in the side with an arrow. The fox yelped in pain and disappeared into the brush. The samurai continued on his way, but a few minutes later saw the same fox again, limping in front of him. Ready to finish it off, the samurai unslung his bow, but the animal ducked away into the tall grass and vanished.

At last, when the samurai was almost home, he spotted the fox for a third time. But something was different. It was running toward his house, carrying a mouthful of fire. The samurai spurred on his horse. Still too far away to do anything, he helplessly watched as the fox transformed into a human and set his home ablaze. Riding his horse at full speed, the samurai aimed another arrow at the beast. But before he could shoot, the vulpine arsonist had returned back into a fox and raced away. That night the samurai's house burned to the ground, and he learned a valuable lesson: Don't mess with foxes.

In Modern Stories

The manga *Shaman King* features a red fireball that acts as the character named Millie's Guardian Ghost. Demonstrating the confusion about different kinds of mysterious glowing orbs, this one is called an onibi, but inside the fire is the face of a fox. Another beautifully illustrated manga by the French duo Atelier Sentô is titled *Onibi: Diary of a Yokai Ghost Hunter.*

NOW YOU KNOW

Hitodama (人魂) literally means "human soul" and are a third otherworldly fiery sphere. A hitodama has a wisp-like tail and floats along, sometimes heading toward a temple that the person—while alive—had a strong relationship with. It's also said, if you look closely, you can see the face of the former human inside the incandescent orb.

RAIJIN AND FŪJIN
雷神 and 風神

Pronunciation: RYE-jeen and FOO-jeen

Translation: Thunder and Lightning or Storm God and Wind God

Raijin is also known as: Kaminari-sama (雷様),
Raiden-sama (雷電様), Narukami (鳴神), Raikō (雷公)

Fūjin is also known as: Fūten (風天)

Overview

Raijin and Fūjin are the unmistakable sibling duo that roam the skies, especially during storms. They are both Shinto gods and yōkai, with Raijin being the god of thunder, lightning, and storms and Fūjin being the god of wind. They're easily recognizable: Their hair and long, ribbony pennants blow wildly in the tempest they've created. Barefoot and naked from the waist up, both gods are well-muscled giants, riding on clouds and baring their teeth, looking fierce and resembling oni (see the Oni entry). The two are brothers but also rivals. Some theories state thunderstorms are the result of their fighting; others suggest they work together to create nasty weather.

Though they look similar, Fūjin and Raijin can be told apart. The most iconic piece of artwork of the pair was painted by Tawaraya Sotatsu (1570–1643), and it consists of three golden panels with Fūjin and Raijin on either side, facing each other; it's from this image almost all following depictions derive. It can be seen in the Kyoto National Museum.

When trying to differentiate the two, keep in mind that Raijin's skin is deep red or pale white. He holds a small mallet in each hand, which he uses to beat on the many taiko drums embedded on the ring that surrounds him, causing thunder. He has three fingers, which represent past, present, and future, and two horns on his head. While he is feared, some farmers pray to him for rain or for a lucky lightning strike that will bring a bumper harvest. Raijin has a son named Raitarō and is sometimes seen with the thunder beast (see the Raijū entry).

Fūjin, on the other hand, has blue or green skin and bright red hair and wears a leopard-skin loincloth. He has a single horn jutting from his forehead. In each of his hands, he grasps the ends of what looks like a long piece of white cloth. This is, in fact, a bag of wind that he manipulates to cause great gales. Traditionally, Fūjin has four fingers.

Both Raijin and Fūjin have an interesting backstory. According to the mythology, they were born from the rotting corpse of Izanami, the divine female creator of Japan. Izanagi (Izanami's husband) followed her to the Yomi no Kuni (Land of the Dead) and, after seeing her miserable condition (decaying corpse), fled—but not before a horde of demons started chasing him. Izanagi escaped and blocked the entrance to the underworld with a large stone to stop any demons from getting out. Raijin and Fūjin, however, managed to escape through a crack.

Background and Popular Stories

One particularly disturbing folktale about one of this duo is called the "Legend of Shokuro." Once upon a time, a man named Shokuro lived in the village of Oinura. Shokuro was strong and confident and wanted to impress the magistrate of his district, so he promised him that he would capture the thunder god.

Shokuro had a brilliant idea. Since Raijin adored human belly buttons (see the sidebar), all he needed to do was attach a person's navel to a kite, then fly the kite during a thunderstorm. Surely Raijin—out and active because of the weather—would snap up the bait and be caught.

There was only one problem: How could Shokuro obtain a human belly button? The answer came while he was out strolling in the woods one day and met a woman named Ochiyo; he callously killed her and cut out the required body part. He then disposed of her body in a ditch.

Soon after this incident, Raijin was passing by overhead and noticed the poor dead woman. He came down to investigate. The thunder god was dazzled by her beauty but alarmed that she was missing her navel. But that wasn't a problem. He just happened to be chewing on some other person's belly button at the time, so he took it out of his mouth and gave it to Ochiyo, thus bringing her back to life. The two had an instant connection; Raijin swept her up into the skies and they were soon married.

A few days later, Shokuro was still out hunting for the god of thunder and lightning. Ochiyo, who was now living in the clouds with her new husband, noticed his kite and went over to check it out. But as she neared, she recognized Shokuro as her murderer. At the same time, Shokuro, too, realized whose attention he'd caught with his morbid kite trap. Ochiyo reclaimed her own navel just as Raijin swooped down from the heavens to take vengeance on the man who had initially killed his newly revived wife.

Shokuro was very strong; surprisingly, he severely beat Raijin. Afterward, the remorseful Shokuro begged Ochiyo's forgiveness, which she accepted before returning to the heavens with her husband. The magistrate, along with the entire village, were awed by Shokuro, and he went on to become quite famous, which was his original goal all along.

In Modern Stories

This dynamic duo has inspired many characters in current pop culture. For example, in the manga and anime *Naruto*, both Naruto and Sasuke show the telltale signs of the mythical duo: They're rivals, and Naruto controls the winds and Sasuke controls lightning. They also take on the criminals named Raijin and Fūjin, who are also known as the Legendary Stupid Brothers.

In the video game *Mortal Kombat*, Raiden (another name for Raijin) is the god of thunder. Raiden also shows up in *Metal Gear Solid*. Raijin and Fūjin are portrayed in *Final Fantasy VIII* as well. Here, Fūjin is female and wearing all blue, and the character on her pauldron means "wind." Raijin is a muscular male, and the character on his shoulder guard means "thunder."

Pokémon's Tornadus and Thundurus are also inspired by the god of thunder and god of wind.

NOW YOU KNOW

In Japan, when children hear thunder, they're told to cover up their belly buttons, or else Raijin will come and steal it away or eat it. Some versions of this superstition state that it isn't Raijin but his little pet friend raijū (see the Raijū entry for more) that is the real danger. When the raijū runs off, he sometimes decides to curl up in random navels to nap. This incurs the thunder god's wrath—and a lightning bolt aimed at a belly button hurts. The real reason for the superstition might be simply to get children to keep their tummies warm when there are sudden drops in temperature due to storms.

RAIJŪ
雷獣

Pronunciation: RYE-joo

Translation: Thunder Beast or Thunder Animal

Overview

The raijū is a yōkai related to thunder, lightning, and storms—in fact, some legends state that it is entirely composed of lightning. It's smaller, more frenetic, and much more difficult to identify than the similar and better-known thunder and storm god, Raijin (see the Raijin and Fūjin entry). It's been reported to live above the clouds or deep in the mountains. Wherever it resides, this mysterious and volatile brute unleashed a considerable amount of mayhem during the Edo era (1603–1867), and stories abound to chronicle it.

Descriptions about what the raijū actually looks like are numerous and diverse. It seems to have appeared in various animal guises—oftentimes bizarre ones at that.

You'll frequently see it as a blue and white wolf enveloped in a web of lightning. But there are also tales of it looking like a puppy, tanuki (Japanese racoon dog), cat, weasel, squirrel, seahorse, crab, or tangled ball of lightning, just to name a few. When it appears in an animal shape, it typically has long inward-curving claws, webbed fingers, and fangs.

Some descriptions come from written works, such as the prolific author Kyokutei Bakin's book *Gendō Hōgen* (玄同放言). There the raijū resembles a wolf with two front legs, four hind legs, and a split tail (like a nekomata—see the Bakeneko and Nekomata entry). *Sunkoku Magazine* (駿国雑誌), which was published in the mid-1800s, reported there was a raijū living on Takakusayama (高草山) in present-day Fujieda City, Shizuoka Prefecture, that was about 24 inches (60 centimeters) long and resembled a weasel or a cat. It had long reddish-black fur with black dots, round eyes, small round ears like those of a mouse, a very long tail, and claws. During thunderstorms, this raijū could be seen riding on clouds and accidentally crashing into trees, breaking them apart, as well as harming anyone who happened to be nearby.

Background and Popular Stories

Raijū are often seen in the company of the thunder and storm god, Raijin. It seems the thunder beasts are sort of pets to Raijin. There is one problem with their friendship, though—how Raijin wakes the raijū up. It's a mystery how it's done, but raijū like to nestle and sleep in people's belly buttons. When Raijin wants to rouse a raijū and call it back to him, he shoots lightning arrows at his little friend. The unfortunate outcome of this method is grave injury to the sleeping human.

Much like the accounts of its appearance, tales of the raijū are also plentiful and varied. Most of the time, raijū are quiet and harmless, but when weather turns foul, they get agitated and start zooming around. They can ride down to Earth on a peal of thunder or streak of lightning or in a ball of fire. Then they start jumping around frantically from tree to tree, around fields, and even between buildings, wreaking havoc as they do. Have you ever seen a tree scarred by a lightning strike? That is actually a vicious scratch from a raijū's long claws. Then there are tales of them just dropping out of the sky during a storm.

There are also legends of raijū living in the mountains. In *Ehon Hyaku Monogatari* (絵本百物語), or the *Picture Book of a Hundred Stories* (1841), in a chapter titled "Thunder," there's a story of a raijū that settled in the hills of Tochigi Prefecture. It was usually as docile as a cat, but at the first sign of rain clouds, it would rush into the air and start racing about, full of frenetic energy.

All this racing around destroyed crops and caused a lot of damage. If lightning struck a particular rice field, the townspeople would immediately erect a tall bamboo pole decorated with sacred shimenawa ropes at the spot. This would keep the raijū from descending again and bringing any more devastation. This story is especially interesting because in other places in Japan, a lightning strike to a field was thought to be a *lucky* event. Superstition said it reenergized the soil and brought abundant harvests. There's even an old saying: "Kaminari ga ōi to hōsaku ni naru" (雷が多いと豊作になる), which means, "If there is a lot of thunder and lightning, there will be a bountiful harvest."

In the mountains of Tochigi Prefecture, during the summer months, raijū would pop their heads out of holes and gaze up at the sky. Once they found what they were looking for, in a roll of thunder, they'd leap swiftly into the air and jump on top of their favorite suitable cloud.

Finally, some people say that the chimeric nue defeated by Minamoto no Yorimasa (see the Nue entry) was actually a raijū, given they can appear as so many different creatures.

There are many folktales involving the raijū—this one involves a real person and (mostly) real events. Once, there lived a great samurai named Tachibana Dōsetsu (1513–1585) who was in possession of a famed sword called Chidori (千鳥), or One Thousand Birds. Dōsetsu was out one day when he decided to rest under a tree and cool off from the summer heat. Suddenly, the skies grew dark and foreboding, and a crackle of lightning exploded very close to him. Dōsetsu withdrew Chidori and, with unimaginable speed, sliced through the thunderbolt, saving his own life and leaving dead on the ground a smoldering raijū. He soon renamed his sword from One Thousand Birds to Raikiri (雷切), or Lightning Cutter.

Unfortunately, the incident left Dōsetsu's left leg paralyzed. As a testament to the man's bravery and determination, Dōsetsu didn't let a partially incapacitated body stop him. This legend still went on to fight another thirty-seven battles, charging in on a horse, always with Raikiri by his side.

In Modern Stories

In the anime *Inuyasha*, the Thunder (Beast) Brothers, Hiten and Manten, are called Raijū Brothers in Japanese. Another interesting sighting is in the manga and anime *Naruto*. In it, there are techniques called Chidori and Raikiri, referencing Tachibana Dōsetsu's legendary sword. And in the movie *Pacific Rim* (2013), one of the giant monster kaijus is called Raiju.

Beyond anime and film, you can find many riffs on the raijū in the Pokémon pantheon. A few are: Raikou, Jolteon, Manectric, Luxray, Zeraora, and let's not forget Raichu and the king of all Pokémon, Pikachu itself.

NOW YOU KNOW

The mummified remains of reported raijū still exist in museums across Japan. In addition, there are quite a few records of people who captured raijū, some of whom even raised them. One particular story mentioned that the creature ate small insects and eggs and loved corn. It's generally believed that an animal called the hakubishin, or masked palm civet, was first introduced to Japan after World War II, but some theorize this animal arrived earlier, during the Edo era (1603–1867). Perhaps it was these peculiar-looking new animals, which lived in trees, acted nervously during storms, occasionally plummeted from the branches, and had a fondness for corn, that were mistaken for the thunder beast.

ROKUROKUBI
ろくろ首

Pronunciation: ROH-koo-roh-koo-bee

Translation: The Long-Necked Woman

Etymology: A *rokuro* is a kind of pulley that expands and contracts. *Kubi* means "neck" or "head."

Similar to: Nukekubi (抜け首), a similar yōkai with a detachable head; Mikoshi Nyūdō (神輿入道), a very tall, bald male yōkai with an ever-extending neck

---

Overview

The rokurokubi is a very unsettling yōkai, dating back to the 1600s. It looks like a normal person—who knows, it could even be your best friend! What usually happens though, either purposefully or while asleep, the human-looking rokurokubi's neck mysteriously elongates. It snakes about the room, sometimes even out the window and down the street, with its head bobbing at the end. Most of the time, it's looking for something to eat. Rokurokubi are usually female, but not always.

The morning after the neck stretching and food hunting, that same rokurokubi often has no memory of what happened the night before. It's said maybe the poor soul doesn't even realize they are afflicted with the condition. At least one tale reports of someone who only discovered their awful state after they kept waking up with an inexplicably full stomach. (That's a little revolting, given that when a rokurokubi goes out after dark, they like to feast on grubs and other insects. If they're near the ocean, they'll prowl the shore in search of crabs.)

There have also been stories of men who visited the pleasure quarters of old Japan and woke up in the middle of the night to find their companion's body still sleeping beside them, yet her head—attached to a long wormy neck—was over on the other side of the room, licking the sardine oil from an andon lamp.

There is a related yōkai called a nukekubi, on the other hand, which has a detachable head and is a little more aggressive. Instead of dreamily chomping on bugs, it flies around at night either alone or in a pack; when feeling a little peckish, some suggest this creature hunts for human flesh. There is a way to defeat a nukekubi, though. All you need to do is hide its body when it isn't looking. The head will return before dawn and, unable to find its lower half, will wail and fly about and eventually knock itself against the floor three times until it's dead.

Background and Popular Stories

Lafcadio Hearn, in his 1904 book *Kwaidan: Stories and Studies of Strange Things*, penned the following well-known story about this yōkai, called "Rokuro-Kubi." Hearn calls the yōkai in his story a rokurokubi, however, the monsters he describes sound and act more like nukekubi. (Some think that Hearn might have mixed up the two upon hearing the tale originally, or that there are regional differences.)

Nearly five hundred years ago, after losing his daimyo (lord) in battle, a great samurai changed his name to Kairyō and became a traveling Buddhist monk. The heart of a samurai still beating bravely in his chest, he decided to spread the word of the Buddha by visiting places all other monks dared not go.

One evening, Kairyō found himself in the hills with no town in sight and decided to settle down and sleep by the side of the road. Soon, though, a woodcutter came along and insisted he return with him to his humble home, as this area was filled with dreadful beasts that did terrible things at night. Kairyō accepted the offer.

He was then introduced to four other men and women living in a small house. He learned the woodcutter, too, used to be a great samurai, but his bad judgment and misdeeds regrettably led him to this life of poverty. Kairyō commiserated and, after being shown to a small side room to sleep, promised to recite sutras so that the Buddha might better the woodcutter's fortune. The monk prayed long into the night.

Eventually, he grew thirsty and snuck out to get some water. Was he ever surprised to find the five sleeping bodies in the main room headless! But there was no blood. A quick investigation proved what he suspected. He'd been lured to the cottage of a rokurokubi. First, Kairyō threw the woodcutter's body out the window, then he went in search of the monsters.

In a nearby grove, he hid and watched as the five floating heads chatted about how they wished the traveling monk would hurry and sleep so they could eat him. They couldn't touch him while he prayed. It was almost morning, they were hungry, and they'd soon have to return to their bodies. One of the women's heads flitted back to check.

She soon returned, shrieking that not only was their visitor gone, so was the woodcutter's body. The woodcutter howled and vowed revenge. Then, spotting Kairyō, they all attacked. But the monk had armed himself with a sturdy young tree and knocked them about until the woodcutter's friends fled in defeat. The woodcutter's head, though, refusing to give up, continued its assault, finally biting the monk's sleeve and not letting go. Nothing Kairyō did could release the ghoul, which he carried around with him until sometime later, when he sold his jacket to a robber, the lifeless head still attached.

In Modern Stories

You might run across the rokurokubi in the manga *Kanojyo wa Rokurokubi* (*My Girlfriend Is a Rokurokubi*) and in several movies, including *Yokai Monsters: 100 Monsters* (1968), a movie called *Yokai Monsters: Spook Warfare* (1968), the 2005 remake *The Great Yokai War*, and its sequel *The Great Yokai War: Guardians* (2021). There's also the Pokémon Misdreavus, which resembles the nukekubi, as it looks like a detached head that flies around.

Rokurokubi and a group of nukekubi even cross cultures to make appearances in the 1998 Hellboy comic book called "Heads," and a pack of seven nukekubi also show up briefly in the animated film entitled *Hellboy: Sword of Storms* (2006).

NOW YOU KNOW

If you suspect someone is a rokurokubi or a nukekubi, look carefully at their neck. Some of these abominable beasts have a thin line, a stretch mark, or light bruising on the skin, indicating it either stretches or comes off. Another hint at identifying one (or determining if *you're* one) is if the person keeps waking up in the morning pleasantly full even though they didn't eat much at dinner the day before, and their burps taste like crickets.

RYŪ

龍

Pronunciation: REE-yoo

Translation: Dragon

Also known as: Tatsu (竜), Orochi (大蛇), Kuraokami (闇淤加美神)

Overview

The ryū, or dragon, a creature of immense power and magnificence, is viewed as a divine kami (god) and has strong ties to both Shinto and Buddhism. This legendary beast has inspired countless folktales and epic encounters as well as literally being present at Japan's mythical beginnings. After the deities Izanagi and Izanami created the islands of Japan, Izanami tragically died from giving birth to the fire god, Kagutsuchi. A furious Izanagi beheaded this matricidal, fiery son and chopped him into pieces. Depending on the version of the story, some part of Kagutsuchi's body (or the blood that pooled at the hilt of Izanagi's sword) transformed into the deity Kuraokami (闇淤加美神), the dragon god of rain and snow.

The first thing you'll notice about Eastern dragons compared to Western ones is that the Eastern variety are more serpentine and have no wings. Wingless though they are, they can still soar into the heavens if they want. Places you can find ryū are oceans, lakes, rivers, and waterfalls. That's because they are associated with water, clouds, and rain.

The *Wakan Sansai Zue* (和漢三才図会), or *Illustrated Sino-Japanese Encyclopedia* (1712) states that Japanese dragons have a head that resembles a horse, eyes of a rabbit, ears of an ox, a tail like a snake, the belly of a dragonfly, scales like a carp, and the claws of a hawk.

That image aside, dragons in Japan aren't evil or necessarily destructive, per se, like Western ones tend to be. The Japanese ryū are instead godly symbols of power and good fortune. Their connection with water (through rainfall) makes them important deities for farmers. Ryū are also tied to fertility, wisdom, and abundance.

Background and Popular Stories

Though ryū aren't inherently evil, that's not to say they aren't extremely dangerous when crossed. The orochi (大蛇), literally "big snake" or "large serpent," are an early kind of dragon that lean more to the malevolent side. As stated in the *Kojiki* (C.E. 712), Yamata no Orochi was an eight-headed, eight-tailed serpent with eyes that were "red like a winter cherry." It was so huge it stretched over eight hills and valleys and grew firs and cypresses on its back.

The dragon is especially significant to the Japanese people for two other important reasons: The ryū is believed to be the ancestor to the first emperor of Japan, and the actual shape of the island chain that is the Japanese archipelago resembles a dragon.

Because a seven-headed naga (snake/dragon) protected the Buddha after he achieved enlightenment, dragons are also seen as protectors of Buddhism. They can be found in sculptures, in paintings on the ceilings, and living in the deep depths of ponds and lakes situated near temples.

As for Shinto, there are shrines dedicated to Ōwatatsumi no kami (大綿津見神)—also called Watatsumi—which translates as "great deity of the sea." It's not uncommon to see a dragon-shaped sculpture dripping water at the temizuya (water-purification pavilion) in front of a shrine.

But of all the dragons in Japan one of the most powerful is probably Ryūjin (龍神)—literally dragon god—sometimes called Ryūō (竜王), dragon king. It is mentioned across legends, myths, and folktales alike. There is even a mysterious dragon god faith based around this divine mythical creature called Ryūjin Shinkō (龍神信仰). Warriors, leaders, businesspeople, politicians, and anyone really can appeal for blessings from Ryūjin—even today by visiting one of the temples or shrines devoted to him. Kifune Shrine and Yasaka Shrine in Kyoto are two of the more famous ones.

The Ryūjin of folk stories, though, lives in a dragon palace called Ryūgū-jō (竜宮城). It is made of red and white coral and is purported to be located somewhere deep in the ocean, floating above it, or near Okinawa. It's a gorgeous magical place where for a human, a single day spent in this palace is something like one hundred years back on Earth. This is substantiated by Urashima Tarō's story.

In the palace, Ryūjin spends his days controlling the tides with his two magical Tide Jewels. A whole host of servants and messengers, including sea turtles, jellyfish, snakes, and the mermaid-ish sea creatures hime-uo and jinja-hime (see the Amabie entry), tend to him.

An often-told children's story called "How the Jellyfish Lost Its Bones" relates to dragon lore. Once upon a time, all jellyfish had bones and even tiny little legs. One such creature was a trusted servant to the dragon god. On a fateful morning, the dragon god's wife fell very ill. The doctors came and did everything they could, but in the end, their consensus was that only a monkey's liver could save her.

There were no monkeys living in the dragon palace or under the sea. So, the dragon god sent the jellyfish to swim to land, find some trees where monkeys lived, and bring him a liver for his beloved wife. The obedient jellyfish set out. Upon finding a monkey, the jellyfish described to it the exquisite dragon god's palace and said that the Ryūjin himself had sent him with an invitation to visit. The monkey was honored and leapt onto the jellyfish's back. Together they swam out into the ocean. After some time, the jellyfish started laughing. When the monkey asked what was so funny, he explained he had tricked the monkey and that the dragon god really just wanted its liver to feed to his ailing wife.

"Oh no," said the monkey. "I left my liver hanging back in the persimmon tree."

Well, that was unexpected. The jellyfish did a quick turnaround and returned to the shore. Once there, the monkey hopped off his back and scampered away, screeching at all its friends to do the same. This time it was the jellyfish that had been tricked. There was nothing he could do—all the monkeys were gone.

The jellyfish returned to the dragon palace in defeat. When the dragon god learned that no liver had been procured, he flew into such a rage that he beat the pitiful animal until he was boneless and a nice jelly consistency—and that's why the jellyfish looks like it does today.

In Modern Stories

Dragons are still everywhere today, from the manga and anime franchise *Dragon Ball*, which started in 1984, to the mobile game *Puzzle & Dragons*. The green and white dragon Haku in Studio Ghibli's 2001 movie *Spirited Away* appears also as a young boy, demonstrating that ryū can sometimes shape-shift into people.

The orochi appears in the 2006 game *Ōkami* as an eight-headed dragon, and also in the manga and anime *One Piece* as both Kurozumi Orochi and Wadatsumi (Dragon King)—the first being mighty and frightening, the other a kind of silly half puffer fish, half man. In *Godzilla: King of the Monsters* (2019), there is mention of a Titan called Yamata no Orochi.

TANUKI

狸

Pronunciation: TAH-noo-key

Translation: Racoon Dog

Also known as: Bakedanuki (化け狸), changing tanuki;
Yōri (妖狸), bewitching or calamitous tanuki; Furudanuki (古狸),
old tanuki (also pronounced Kori); Kairi (怪狸), mysterious tanuki

---

Overview

Tanuki are furry, fluffy-tailed racoon dogs that are both real indigenous animals of Japan and playful jumbo-scrotumed yōkai of lore. A ubiquitous presence throughout Japan's history, they can be found across the entire country in ancient literature, art, and folklore as well as in modern-day children's books, movies, games, and even commercials for instant noodles. Tanuki have a long history in Japan and were written about way back in the *Nihon Shoki* (C.E. 720), which includes a little poem that says, "It's the second month of the year, the time when the tanuki come out in Mutsunokuni [(陸奥国) in northeastern Japan], turn into humans, and sing songs."

Like the kitsune, tanuki are real animals *and* yōkai. Among other special abilities, both creatures, upon reaching a certain venerable age, gain the ability to shape-shift. But there is a difference between the two: Kitsune tend to turn into beautiful women to tempt and lure unaware humans, while tanuki have a much larger repertoire. First off, when it comes to their human form, they'd rather become a monk than an enchanting lady. But tanuki can also switch into various animals, other yōkai, and even inanimate objects.

Tanuki that can shape-shift are called bake-danuki (化け狸). *Bake* is from the verb *bakeru* and means "to change" or "to transform." There's an old saying: "Kitsune nana bake, tanuki ya bake" (狐七化け、狸八化け), which means, "Foxes can change form seven times, tanuki can transform eight." In terms of Japanese folklore, that puts tanuki on a higher level than the kitsune when it comes to shape-shifting. One technique used for transforming is to place a special leaf on their heads.

Tanuki are mostly charming comedians in the pantheon. This is evidenced by their magical ability to make you see what they want you to see. For example, while in the form of a monk, one might offer you money—but when you try to spend it later, it will turn out to be dried leaves or animal dung. Despite these tricks, they very rarely cause much harm and only wish to tease and play pranks on people.

Background and Popular Stories

Though they are merry pranksters, tanuki are also considered lucky. You can find statues of them in front of temples, businesses, and private homes all over Japan.

Of these statues, Shiga Prefecture produces probably the most popular stoneware pottery version of the raccoon dog called Shigaraki (信楽) tanuki. This much-loved figure came about in the late nineteenth century, when one night, a famous potter named Fujiwara Tetsuzo witnessed a tanuki in the moonlight drumming out music on its fat belly. This behavior is often ascribed to the party-loving racoon dog, but for Fujiwara to witness the event was truly auspicious. Afterward, he decided to make some tanuki statues and share the good luck with others.

The Shigaraki tanuki is distinguishable by its eight lucky parts: smiling face (to bring happiness), conical sedge hat (to protect against trouble), big belly (for bold and calm decisiveness), big eyes (to see things clearly to make the right decisions), sake jug (to have enough food and drink and be sociable), bank book (symbolizing trust, built up little by little, like your savings), big tail (to be stable and end things well), and let's not forget the large testicles (representing money; the bigger the better—more on these next).

One thing that is hard to miss about the bake-danuki is its ridiculously endowed scrotum—it's on all the statues, images, and figurines. Though it seems obscene, it, too, is considered fortuitous. Ages ago, goldsmiths would place gold nuggets (called kintama, which is also the name for "testicles" in Japanese) between tanuki pelts to hammer out gold leaf. The idea of stretching a small piece of gold and the tanuki skin became enmeshed, and thus the animal's auspicious body part was born.

In old woodblock artwork, you can find the tanuki playfully and unbelievably stretching these elephantine testicles into incredible sizes and shapes. They were turned into everything from hats and blankets to nets—some tanuki would even paint a face on them and dress them in a nice kimono to shock some unwary victim. Perhaps a little of that special tanuki magic that makes you see what the racoon dog wants you to see (like the leaf money previously mentioned) is involved in these shenanigans. There is even a popular children's song ("Tan Tan Tanuki") that references the animal's large naughty bits and how they sway back and forth, *bura bura*, even if there's no breeze. Ironically, it's sung to the Christian hymn "Shall We Gather at the River?"

In addition to being part of everyday life, tanuki are present in folktales as well. One of the most famous stories about the tanuki is called "Bunbuku Chagama," or "The Accomplished and Lucky Tea Kettle" or "The Wonderful Tea Kettle." There are many different versions, but here's a popular one.

Once upon a time, a kindly, poor man was trekking through the woods when he came across a tanuki caught in a hunter's trap. He immediately freed the sorry creature and watched it scamper off. A short while later, he came upon a splendid chagama (cast iron tea kettle) in the middle of the path. The man wondered who would leave such a magnificent thing out here to rust in the elements, and he took it home.

For some odd reason, he felt affection for this kettle, but it was much too fancy for him to keep, so he gave it to the head monk of the local temple. The head monk was also impressed with the object. He thanked the man and asked him to at least sit down and share a cup of tea. The monk filled the tea kettle with water and set it above the hot coals.

Almost at once, it began to sweat and tremble. Then the kettle let out a scream and with a *pop!* it sprouted a bushy tail, four legs, and a tanuki's head! It then leapt off the fire and rolled around on the floor in pain. The kindly, poor man felt terrible and begged to keep the half-metamorphosed tea kettle tanuki so that he could nurse it back to health. The monk agreed.

It turns out that this was the same tanuki the man had saved earlier. It had transformed into the tea kettle as a way to repay the old man—only evidently it didn't foresee that in tea kettle form, it might at some point be placed on a fire. Over time, the half kettle, half tanuki healed, but it never changed completely back to a racoon dog. It decided to live with the kindly, poor man. But it had an idea: Instead of being poor, why didn't they work up some kind of entertaining performance and charge people to watch the strange creature and his new friend? That's exactly what they did, and then they weren't poor anymore. It truly was a wonderful and lucky tea kettle.

In Modern Stories

Tanuki might be just as pervasive outside Japan as they are inside. The most iconic gathering of tanuki is Studio Ghibli's movie *Pom Poko* (1994), but there are more. In the manga and anime *Inuyasha*, the character Hachiemon is actually a raccoon dog, as is Tom Nook in the game *Animal Crossing*. Don't forget Mario's flying tanooki suit in *Super Mario Bros. 3* and other variations in the *Super Mario* series. He even uses the leaf!

TENGU

天狗

Pronunciation: TEN-goo

Translation: Mountain Goblin,
(literally) Heaven or Heavenly Dog

Overview

Tengu are majestic, powerful, frightening, and utterly cool mountain-dwelling yōkai with a long and rich backstory. The characters for tengu (天狗) come from the Chinese word *tiangou*, which means "heavenly dog" or "celestial dog." There are several origin stories about this yōkai, but one states that in ancient times, some kind of meteor blazed across the sky, made a loud noise like a barking dog, and soon afterward bad luck and even a war ensued.

Thanks to their association with the meteor, for hundreds of years, tengu were thought to be harmful spirits that caused illness, misfortune, and bloodshed. In the eleventh-century work *The Tale of Genji*, the tengu were mentioned as fearsome goblins that played tricks and abducted people. Over time, though, that reputation evolved. By the Heian era (C.E. 794–1185), they began taking on birdlike qualities, ranging from those of the tobi or tonbi (black kite) to the buzzard. After that came the red-faced tengu that is so popular today. Interestingly, despite the name "heavenly dog," tengu never really had a doglike appearance in Japan.

There are generally believed to be two types of tengu:

1. The karasu tengu (烏天狗), or crow tengu, also called the kotengu (小天狗), meaning "small tengu" or "lesser tengu." As the name suggests, these tengu resemble crows or other birds of prey. They're contentious and dangerous but not as strong as the second category of tengu. Some depictions of the crow tengu look quite similar to the Indian god Garuda. There are those who believe this Hindu deity inspired the looks of this early tengu. Gradually, it morphed into the second type.

2. The hanadaka tengu (鼻高天狗) (long- or high-nosed tengu), also called ōtengu (大天狗), meaning "great(er) tengu," or daitengu (same characters). You see this kind more often these days. They have crimson faces, long noses, white hair and beards, and great big wings on their backs. Ōtengu are much larger and more commanding and wield greater magical powers than the smaller, more primitive crow variety.

You might find both species wearing yamabushi, or mountain ascetic, robes (recognizable because they have six fluffy pom-poms decorating them, four in the front and two in the back); small, black, box-like caps called tonkin that are tied to their foreheads; and on their feet, high, single-toothed geta shoes. They are often holding staffs, swords, naginata, or fans made from either feathers or a large leaf called a yatsude.

Background and Popular Stories

The tengu have both Shinto and Buddhists roots. On the Shinto side, they are considered kami (gods). The long-nosed Sarutahiko Ōkami, Shinto deity

of the crossroads, looks incredibly similar and is considered the inspiration for the hanadaka tengu.

In Buddhism, however, tengu were at first believed to be harbingers of doom and evil and entities that acted as nemeses to the Buddhist way because they were too prideful. This thought eventually evolved, and there came the idea that there were both good and bad tengu. The good ones were the reincarnations of monks who had reached enlightenment, died, and returned. However, holy men who led less-than-holy lives or harbored feelings of selfishness, greed, and anger—and especially those who were arrogant and vain—were reborn as the bad kind of tengu. In keeping with that association of tengu being prideful, there is a phrase in Japan, "tengu ni naru" (天狗になる), which is used to refer to someone who is overly confident and big-headed.

Slowly, however, the tengu's image began to change again and took on a protecting presence. The eighteenth-century book *Kaidan Toshiotoko* (怪談登志男) describes the tengu looking like a yamabushi (mountain ascetic) and serving the head monk in a Zen temple. These formidable beasts then started to become protectors of mountains, with many sacred peaks all over Japan still believed to be occupied by certain individual tengu.

Tengu are also highly skilled martial artists. A tengu named Sōjōbō trained the famous samurai Minamoto no Yoshitsune and taught him swordsmanship as a child so, once older, the samurai could avenge his father's death.

In addition, tengu are proficient in many types of magic and sorcery, such as shape-shifting, showing humans phantom scenery, or giving them sweets that are actually horse dung in disguise. They can also create illusionary sounds like birds or trees falling and crashing in the forest. Another little trick they can perform to warn intruders off their mountains is called tengu tsubute (天狗礫), where they rain down sand or pebbles that mysteriously disappear before they hit the ground. Tengu can even read people's minds, predict the future, and, with a wave of their fans, stir up great gusts of wind or tempests. They can also start fires or extinguish them.

Then there is teleportation. Another distinctly tengu trait is kamikakushi (神隠し), literally translated as "hidden by the gods," though in English it's conveyed as "spirited away." It's also sometimes referred to as "tengu sarai," which means "stolen or swept away by a tengu." And that's exactly what happens: Kamikakushi is how people used to explain sudden and mysterious disappearances of children and sometimes even adults. This phenomenon occurred for centuries. Blaming a tengu for snatching up a child who might have wandered into the woods or fallen into a river gave the distraught parents somewhere to direct their anguish, and also provided them some hope—the child might just return.

The extraordinary thing is that sometimes the child did. If the abductee was fortunate enough to be returned home, there were several outcomes. Certain little ones had no memory of what had happened, others had developed a mental disability, while still others told stories of wondrous journeys to faraway places and flying through the air. In some accounts, people even reported being flown to the moon.

In Modern Stories

There is an abundance of tengu in manga, anime, and games. A few places you might have seen one, though, are the Pokémon Nuzleaf and Shrifty; in the manga and anime *Demon Slayer* as Urokodaki Sakonji, a master swordsman; and in the game *Ghost of Tsushima*. *Spirited Away* (2001), by Studio Ghibli, is called *Sen to Chihiro no Kamikakushi* in Japanese, however, no tengu appear in the movie. Tengu even have their own emoji—it's the angry red-faced creature with the long nose.

TŌFU KOZŌ

豆腐小僧

Pronunciation: TOH-foo KOH-zoh

Translation: Tofu Boy

Similar to: Hitotsume Kozō (一つ目小僧)

Overview

The tōfu kozō is an endearing, timid boy-looking yōkai who simply wishes to give you a gift, a block of tofu. He's recognizable not only by the bean curd–topped tray he's carrying but also by his signature style. He is frequently depicted with an oversized bald head and dressed in a kimono, wooden geta shoes, and a traditional wide-brimmed hat called a kasa. He comes out on rainy days and can be seen standing in the street or following people around, trying to ply them with tofu.

Some artists' interpretations depict him with a single giant eye and dangling tongue, which is probably why he's at times linked to, or confused with, the hitotsume kozō (see the Hitotsume Kozō entry). There are also prints that show him with feet that have two long claws, suggesting that he's not a normal little boy, while in others he's carrying a jug of sake too.

The tōfu kozō doesn't shape-shift or hide any bloodthirsty intentions; if anything, he's a little bullied himself. Even though his parents are rumored to be a rokurokubi (a humanlike creature that can stretch its neck—see the Rokurokubi entry) and a mikoshi nyūdō (another long-necked yōkai), he's often portrayed as a servant or underling to stronger yōkai, who tend to push him around. This might explain the sake too: He's serving them.

The interesting thing about the tōfu kozō is that in the grand scheme of Japanese supernatural beings, this bean curd giver isn't very old, compared to many that were written about in the *Kojiki* (C.E. 712) and *Nihon Shoki* (C.E. 720). The innocent-enough-looking creature appeared out of nowhere sometime in the late 1700s then again at the end of the Edo era (1603–1867) through to the Meiji era (1868–1912). Nevertheless, he was hugely popular, showing up in books—especially yellow-covered books called kibyōshi (黄表紙), picture books produced from 1175 to the early nineteenth century that were considered comic books for adults—poetry, and kabuki performances and even illustrated on all kinds of toys, like kites, board games, and cards.

Remember that gift he wants to give you? The tofu is called momiji-dōfu (紅葉豆腐) and is usually marked with a small crimson-colored maple leaf. Later, in the Showa (1926–1989) and Heisei (1989–2019) eras, the tale evolved to add that if you accept this block of tofu and then are foolish enough to take a bite from it, mold will start growing all over your body.

Background and Popular Stories

The tōfu kozō is also reportedly connected to epidemics of smallpox in Japanese history. The first recorded case of smallpox in Japan was in C.E. 735 During a three-year period from C.E. 735–737, this previously unseen disease killed approximately a third of the population. At the beginning, it was presumed to be onryō, or vengeful spirits. But eventually, a new kami (god) was born. The hōsōgami or hōsōshin (疱瘡神) manifested from the need to understand and explain these unfathomable happenings. The Japanese characters literally mean "smallpox god"; however, in English, this kami is sometimes called the smallpox demon or devil, for obvious reasons.

During the Edo era (1603–1867), this dreadful and deadly disease was still running rampant, and science and medicine weren't yet able to explain and deal with it. No one knew what caused the illness or how to cure it, but by then they had been living with it for hundreds of years. By this time, it had become a childhood disease, as adults who survived smallpox were immune. Children, though, were particularly vulnerable and were often scarred or, if it affected the eyes, blinded.

In houses and towns everywhere, the hōsōgami was both feared and prayed to in turn. People wanted to drive it away or appease its wrath— whichever worked. One way to do that was through the use of folk medicine, which included dances, exorcisms, the color red, and using special imagery. This imagery included legendary warriors like Momotarō and Kintarō (see their entries) as well as toys like horned owls, daruma dolls (legless dolls that depict the Bodhidharma—founder of Zen Buddhism—and represent perseverance), den-den drums (small handheld drums you rotate to make the attached beaded strings strike the drums, as seen in *The Karate Kid Part II*), and tai fish–shaped carts (tai fish, or sea bream, were associated with good luck).

So what is the connection between tōfu kozō and smallpox? Some historians, looking closely at the old artwork of the tōfu kozō, noticed that the prints and patterns on his clothes were often the same as the ones used for expelling the hōsōgami. There were daruma dolls, horned owls, drums, and the red tai fish. This has led them to think the tōfu kozō might have been created as a means of protection against smallpox. On the other hand, it also could have been some kind of parody, since the kibyōshi (comic) books that first depicted the tōfu kozō were aimed at adults and usually filled with satire.

In Modern Stories

The anime *Little Ghostly Adventures of Tofu Boy* features as its protagonist a tōfu kozō who is transported to the modern era. Then there are appearances in the role-playing game *Genshin Impact*, the manga and anime *GeGeGe no Kitarō*, and the *Yo-kai Watch* games (as Tofupyon). And in *Nura: Rise of the Yokai Clan* he shows up alongside an entirely new yōkai called Natto Kozō (Fermented Soy Bean Boy).

TSUCHIGUMO

土蜘蛛

Pronunciation: TSOO-chi-GOO-moh

Translation: Earth or Dirt Spider

Also known as: Yatsukahagi (八握脛), Eight Gripping Legs;
Ōgumo (大蜘蛛), Big Spider; Yamagumo (山蜘蛛),
Mountain Spider

Overview

Tsuchigumo are monster spiders that kill. Similar to other real animals in Japan that live inordinately long lives and then mysteriously turn into yōkai (like the kitsune), these eight-legged crawlies can change into giant foul-tempered beasts. The early-fourteenth-century *Tsuchigumo Sōshi* (土蜘蛛草子), or *Picture Scroll of an Earth Spider*, depicts the epic battle between renowned samurai Minamoto no Yorimitsu and one of these cave-dwelling creatures. Various texts through the ages explain legends of battles as well as lists of curiously specific names of individual dirt spiders.

These lists are less eyebrow raising when you realize a second theory is that they aren't old spiders that transformed into jumbo arachnids but were real people. In earlier times, the word *tsuchigumo* was a derogatory term used to describe disloyal local clans. The word might have come from *tsuchi-gomori*, which means "hiding in the earth," as evidenced by these mavericks who refused to obey the imperial court and lived in caves. They were said to have small bodies but very long arms and legs. Some were rumored to have tails, some of which glowed. This rebel tribe were thought to have shamanistic abilities and were considered uncivilized.

So reviled were these tsuchigumo that there are tales of the first emperor, Jimmu, capturing, killing, and chopping up one (or a band of them) and burying the pieces in different places. It's unclear whether the enemy he destroyed was the mythical spider or an Indigenous clan of people called the Katsuragi, who lived in that area, were nicknamed "tsuchigumo," and suffered greatly at the hands of the emperor. A clue, though, is that tsuchigumo only started to be described as giant spiders around the twelfth century, about 1,700 years after Emperor Jimmu eradicated the tsuchigumo.

Background and Popular Stories

Minamoto no Yorimitsu (源頼光) (C.E. 948–1021), who also went by the name Minamoto no Raikō, was a famed samurai who served under the regents of the Fujiwara clan. You may remember him from the entry on Kintarō, when he ran across the young marvel and asked him to join his four legendary devoted followers dubbed Shitennō (四天王), or Four Heavenly Kings. Minamoto no Yorimitsu is connected to quite a few heroic battles against mythical beasts and yōkai.

The tale of the battle between Yorimitsu and a tsuchigumo has been told and retold, and many versions exist. It's been turned into a Noh play and performed on the Kabuki stage (both versions eponymously named *Tsuchigumo*). The story usually goes like this.

Once upon a time, Minamoto no Yorimitsu suddenly fell very ill for no apparent reason. As he was usually so strong and full of vigor, his condition baffled everyone. There was nothing he could do but rest.

Late one night, he woke a little delirious from fever and saw by the paper lantern light a priest sitting beside his futon. They exchange a little conversation, and even though he was feeling unwell and his mind was foggy,

Yorimitsu could sense something was off about this man. This priest was unexpectedly dark in color and larger than a real person. That's when Yorimitsu realized it wasn't a priest at all. It was a giant tsuchigumo!

The spider, sensing it had been found out, spit a spray of webs from its mouth at the prone warrior. But Minamoto no Yorimitsu was no fool. He slept with his cherished sword, Hizamaru, tucked under his futon. With a swift movement, he sliced through the webs, hitting and injuring the spider/priest. Yorimitsu collapsed and the monster fled.

The next day, Yorimitsu, still not well but determined to finish off the tsuchigumo that he thought had attempted to murder him in his sleep, rose and called his comrades, the Shitennō. Together, the five samurai followed the bloody trail left by the spider beast. It led all the way to Mount Katsuragi in Nara Prefecture.

There they found the enormous tsuchigumo waiting for them. They learned it was hundreds of years old and was harboring a grudge. This tsuchigumo was actually an onryō (angry spirit) of those original local clans that had been wiped out by Emperor Jimmu so many years in the past. It was also the tsuchigumo that was making Minamoto no Yorimitsu sick.

Together the warriors battled the giant beast, which had very long legs and shot both webs and poison from its mouth. Finally, Yorimitsu epically decapitated the tsuchigumo. Another slice of a blade split open its stomach, and out poured 1,990 skulls—its many victims.

Yorimitsu immediately felt better; the curse had been lifted. He renamed his sword from Hizamaru to Kumokiri (蜘蛛切), or Spider Cutter, and the yōkai aberration was cut into pieces (head, body, and legs), each piece being buried separately from the others, similar to what Emperor Jimmu did back in his time. This method was thought to avoid any future curse the creature might enact. One noted place of burial is Katsuragi Hitokotonushi Shrine in Nara. If you go there today, you can still find a stone marked "Kumozuka" (蜘蛛塚), which is the spider's grave.

As for the sword renamed Kumokiri, it, too, is still in existence, although it has changed names again and again through time, and its lineage becomes confusing. There are now three swords that claim to be the original.

In Modern Stories

The earth spider isn't dead yet in popular culture, at least. You can find the Tsuchigumo Clan in the manga and anime *Naruto*, where it even has a small fort on Mount Katsuragi. In the manga and anime *Nurarihyon no Mago*, Tsuchigumo is a well-muscled man with multiple arms. A massive spider appears in several episodes of the anime *Detective Conan*.

TSUCHINOKO

槌の子

Pronunciation: TSOO-chee-noh-koh

Translation: Child of the Mallet or Hammer

Also known as: Tsuchinoko has over forty different names across Japan. Some of the cuter variations are Bachihebi (バチヘビ), Nozuchi (ノヅチ), and Tsuchimbo (ツチンボ).

Overview

The tsuchinoko is both a yōkai and a cryptid (an animal that may exist but has not yet been scientifically verified). It looks like a very short, very thick-in-the-middle snake, but with a tiny little tail. You'll also hear some ancient accounts stating that this legendary beastie has no eyes, nose, or limbs—just that interesting physique and a mouth. (Its name makes sense when you compare its body shape to that of an old-fashioned Japanese mallet, called a yokozuchi. A yokozuchi, used to thresh rice or beat fabric, has a wide round part for pounding and a very short handle.) This beastie's main purpose is just to frighten you and watch you fall down.

The tsuchinoko was mentioned in both the *Kojiki* (written in the year C.E. 712), where it was called Kayano Hime no Kami, and again in the *Nihon Shoki* (C.E. 720), where it was referred to as Kusano Oya Kayano Hime. Both names basically mean "Goddess of the Grass." The artist Toriyama Sekien made a woodblock print of one of these chubby creepers and called it a nozuchi (野槌), or "field hammer."

The tsuchinoko's attack is usually reported like this: You're out hiking in the woods of Japan when you hear an unsettling *cheee!* noise. Next, you notice some rustling in the bushes up ahead. Before you can even turn around and run, out rolls a creature that looks like a short, very wide snake. But instead of slithering as snakes are wont to do, it has its tail clenched in its mouth and is rolling, end over end, toward you at a disturbingly high speed. This method of attack comes with one drawback: it can't change directions quickly. If you need to escape a quick-rolling tsuchinoko, just wait until the last minute and jump out of the way; it will just roll on by.

Tsuchinoko are said to inhabit the mountains and forests all over Japan, except for Hokkaido and some smaller islands. Despite countless comical sightings and harrowing encounters throughout the years, there's no proof one has been captured—though there are some convincing fakes out there.

Background and Popular Stories

There aren't a ton of stories, per se, about the tsuchinoko, but there are a lot of observations by those who have encountered them. For example, people have reported the following:

- Tsuchinoko have eyelids, whereas snakes don't.
- There are varying accounts, but a general consensus is that they can leap 16 feet (5 meters) into the air, while springing forward about 7 feet (2 meters).
- They enjoy imbibing Japanese sake.
- Females have spaces between their teeth.
- They're incredibly fast.

- They have different ways of getting around. For example, in addition to rolling at you like a hoop, they can slither like a snake, crawl forward like an inchworm, and roll sideways like a short log.
- They snore.
- They favor the scents of miso, dried squid, and burning hair.
- Some say they're extremely poisonous.
- Some say they talk. When they do talk, they have a propensity to lie.

Tsuchinoko have numerous nicknames depending on the area. One such name is "tatekurikaeshi," which literally means "stand up and turn around," referring to their end-over-end rolling technique.

Relatively recently, the tsuchinoko has also become somewhat of an urban legend. In 1972, author Seiko Tanabe wrote a serialized novel in the *Asahi Shimbun* newspaper called *Subete Koronde*. It followed a protagonist who was a tsuchinoko enthusiast. A year later, the story was turned into a national public broadcasting–produced drama. Then in 1973, manga artist Takao Yaguchi wrote *Phantom Monster Bachihebi* about a tsuchinoko. The year after that, in 1974, the much beloved anime *Doraemon* came out with an episode about finding one. So, after three years of pop-culture presence, a fad was born, and people began searching for them everywhere. They moved into urban legend territory.

Both Niigata Prefecture and Gifu Prefecture hold unique events celebrating this girthy reptile while at the same time trying to prove its existence. Both festivals are held in May, perhaps because it's spring, so the creatures are active and roaming and no doubt rolling about.

The first one, in Niigata, is called Tsuchinoko Tanken (槌の子探検), which means the Tsuchinoko Hunt. On a chosen day, a large group of participants gather with long-handled nets and cameras to go on a hike, scouring certain mountains and forests, looking for the elusive critters. The second event takes place in Gifu and is called Tsuchinoko Festa (槌の子フェスタ), or Tsuchinoko Festival. Here, again, hundreds of serious hunters are escorted by local guides to areas where one of these slippery serpents might be hiding. Poking around the bushes and tall grass, everyone hopes to uncover a real live tsuchinoko. Regrettably, every year after the events, it's announced that again no fabled beast was spotted or caught.

Even though no one's been able to prove their existence, tsuchinoko remain very popular, with a myriad of merchandise fashioned around them: mascots, cookies, mochi cakes, amulets, keychains, stuffed animals...you name it. But the "kawaii" factor isn't the only thing getting people beating shrubbery with sticks—there's also a reward for finding one! The amount varies depending on the prefecture, but in general, if you nab yourself a real live tsuchinoko, you can receive up to a 1-million-yen reward (about $7,000 US dollars). Some places offer prize money in smaller amounts for a decent photo.

In Modern Stories

Despite the fact that they are so elusive in the wild, you might have heard of or seen one of these stout snakes in Pokémon (Dunsparce), Yu-Gi-Oh!, *Metal Gear Solid*, *Yo-kai Watch* (Shadowside), *Granblue*, and *Monster Hunter*, to name a few places.

TSUKUMOGAMI
付喪神 or 九十九神

Pronunciation: TSOO-koo-moh-GAH-mee

Translation: Very Old Gods or Ninety-Nine-Year-Old Spirits

Also known as: Tool Specters, Haunted Relics,
Ninety-Nine Gods, Artifact Demons

Overview

The term *tsukumogami* doesn't describe one yōkai but is an umbrella term for numerous bizarre beasties, all sharing one thing in common: they were once inanimate objects, but around their one hundredth birthday, or after a very long time, they acquired a soul, or kami, and came to life. Once these objects become sentient, they spend the rest of their time on Earth giving people a good scare or trying to teach them a lesson.

In ancient times, before these silly, creepy, and weird spirit-imbued relics were called tsukumogami, they went by names like:

- Yōbutsu (妖物), or bewitching or calamitous objects
- Kaseinomono (化生のもの), or monstrous things
- Kibutsu no yōhen (器物の妖変), or transformed objects

You can find them depicted in poems, scrolls, paintings, otogizōshi (old short stories from the Muromachi era, 1336–1573), and children's card games called karuta. Some of the more common old-fashioned household appliances, tools, or musical instruments that make the change into yōkai are: futons, straw sandals, saddles and stirrups, scrolls with sutras written on them, mirrors, stringed biwa instruments, prayer beads, kimonos, sake jars, radish graters, and (why not?) mosquito nets. Basically, any old—with the emphasis on *old*—thing can be the receptacle for a soul, given the right conditions.

One of those conditions could be the simple fact that an object reached its magical one hundredth birthday and gained sentience. A second condition occurs when a well-worn object wasn't treated with respect or was callously thrown away. After becoming self-aware, this tsukumogami's purpose is to educate its former owner about the importance of caring for their things.

Despite some past tales of tsukumogami banding together, marching raucously through the streets, and genuinely instilling fear into the people who lived nearby, these days it seems they aren't out to do real harm.

Background and Popular Stories

Tsukumogami are actually connected to housecleaning practices. There is a relatively recent ritual called ōsōji (大掃除), or "big cleaning," that families all across Japan take part in during the last days of December as a way to welcome in the New Year. It's based on an older tradition called susuharai (煤払い), which involved sweeping away the soot from candles, lanterns, and the stove that had accumulated in their homes throughout the year. This practice was believed to banish not only filth but also the bad oni (demons). Ridding yourself of these pesky beasts left room for good kami (gods) to enter your home in the coming year. However, during this cleaning, worn out and broken items from all households were usually left on the roadside or along riverbanks. Imagining all this garbage piled up, you can feel the waste and understand how aggravated these once loved items might become at having been thrown away so heartlessly. The best revenge? Transform into a yōkai!

Here are a few haunted artifacts you might have bumped into before. The karakasa (kasa) obake is an old lacquered umbrella recognizable by its giant lidless eye, long tongue, and single hairy leg, and it hops around wildly. The chōchin obake is a washi paper or silk lantern with a gaping mouth from which you can see an old candle burning inside. Bakezōri are ghost sandals with tiny arms and legs and the often seen single eyeball, and then there's that piece of flying cloth (see the Ittan Momen entry), which is also considered a tsukumogami.

There's only one real way to deal with these meddlesome beasts, and that's by holding a kūyo (供養). A kūyo is a Buddhist or Shinto memorial service where prayers are offered over old, most likely damaged items that a person has relied on and used lovingly for a long period of time. For example, these days, still, kūyo are performed for combs, glasses, dolls, and pins and needles. The ceremony for pins and needles is called hari kūyo. It takes place on a designated day at a designated shrine or temple. Here seamstresses gather and sink all their broken pins and needles into blocks of konnyaku jelly or tofu. Incense is burned, prayers are recited, and the seamstresses press their hands together, give thanks to their tools of the trade, and say goodbye. This is the proper way to guarantee your old things don't come back to haunt you.

In Modern Stories

Various types of tsukumogami appear in manga and anime like *xxxHOLiC*, *GeGeGe no Kitarō*, and *Nura: Rise of the Yokai Clan*. There's also a novel and anime called *Tsukumogami Kashimasu* (meaning, "We Rent Tsukumogami") and its sequel *Tsukumogami, Asobō yo* (meaning, "Let's Play, Tsukumogami"), written by Megumi Hatakenaka. Here, two protagonists work in a secondhand shop where some of the items are actually tsukumogami that help them solve mysteries.

UMIBŌZU

海坊主

Pronunciation: OO-mee-BOH-zoo

Translation: Sea Monk

Also known as: Umihōshi (海坊師), Uminyūdō (海入道)

Overview

The umibōzu are mysterious sea monster yōkai that appear far from shore and have the ability to capsize or sink entire ships, killing everyone on board. Reports vary, but almost all agree they are enormous, dome-shaped black creatures with ill intent. Some accounts say they are smooth and have no faces at all, while others report glowing red eyes and a mouth that stretches from ear to ear. The protruding head-like part of this creature can be many times larger than the boat itself, but there's no way of knowing how big the body extending under the surface of the water is—no one's been brave enough to jump in and see. But the umibōzu aren't always huge—they can be small enough to get caught up in nets too.

Sightings can occur any time of the day or night and in any kind of weather. Although, if one (or more; sometimes they attack in groups) does show itself on a calm day, it will rise up out of the water looking like the shaven head of a monk (hence the name "sea monk"), and the weather will quickly turn rough.

The umibōzu have been feared by sailors for centuries, and there are many illustrations and accounts of run-ins with them. There is an early depiction of one of these sea monsters on a hand scroll from about 1700 called *Bakemono no E* (化け物の絵), or *Illustrated Index of Supernatural Creatures*. This colorful and atypical painting shows a beast with the same smooth bald pate but fins running down its back, a toothy smile, and tentacle-like protrusions snaking from its nose.

The agreed-upon method of escaping a sea monk is for all the sailors to cover their mouths and not make a sound. If the monster hears something, it will immediately destroy the vessel, drowning everyone on board. If the crew are completely silent, then it will pass by. However, it's rumored that just encountering an umibōzu means someone on the boat will die in the near future.

Background and Popular Stories

In old Japan, women were not allowed on ships. Sailors considered the ocean female—a very powerful goddess, if you will, so by inviting a woman aboard, they risked provoking the ocean's jealousy, and that would undoubtedly lead to bad luck at sea, something no sailor wants.

The Edo-era (1603–1867) compilation *Kii Zōdan Shū* (奇異雑談集) was published in 1687 in Kyoto. This collection of strange tales and supernatural phenomena—thought to be a republishing of earlier works—contains this popular story about the umibōzu. Once upon a time, a boat set off from Ise Province (now Mie Prefecture) to Cape Irako. The captain of the ship, as was custom at the time, refused to allow any women to set sail with them. But one of the men, a sailor named Zenchin, snuck his wife aboard. After they got out to sea, the vessel was hit by a violent storm. Zenchin's wife was discovered, and the captain assumed it was having her aboard that angered not the sea itself but the dragon god, Ryūjin (see the Ryū entry), who lived deep in the ocean. In order to appease the disgruntled and tantrum-throwing god, the captain began throwing overboard anything he thought might calm the dangerous deity.

Unfortunately, this didn't work—the storm raged on. Eventually, a creature the story called the kuro nyūdo emerged from the turbulent waters. Its head was six times as big as a human head, and it had glowing eyes and a horse's mouth. Zenchin's wife realized what she had to do and flung herself into the ocean. The kuro nyūdo seized her, and instantly the storm ceased. She had saved the ship and its crew. The kuro nyūdo were said to be dragon gods that had fallen and now swam around demanding sacrifices. Except for the horse's mouth, they sound suspiciously like umibōzu.

Sea monks are among those yōkai that have had more recent sightings too. In 1971, off the coast of Onagawa in Miyagi Prefecture, a fishing boat called the *28th Konpira Maru* suddenly had a fishing line cut, and then a large, wrinkly grayish-brown creature with no mouth surfaced. The startled crew was about to poke it with a harpoon when it vanished under the water.

In Modern Stories

In the manga and anime *Gintama*, Umibōzu is a powerful alien hunter. He's not a sea creature but a human who does end up bald. Interestingly, the kanji for his name has been changed, and the character for "star" is included at the beginning (星海坊主). It doesn't change the pronunciation, but it does make his title as "alien hunter" more appropriate. Another bald human character named Umibōzu can be found in the manga and anime *City Hunter*.

NOW YOU KNOW

Similar but different are funayūrei (船幽霊). They are boat ghosts or vengeful spirits of those who have died at sea and appear during bad weather. They ask you for a bucket or ladle, then use it to fill your boat until it sinks. Give them one with the bottom knocked out to save your life.

URASHIMA TARŌ

浦島太郎

Pronunciation: OO-rah-shee-mah TAH-roh

Also known as: Urashimako (浦島子),
and Urashima no Ko (浦島の子)

Overview

Urashima Tarō is a kindhearted hero from a folk story dating back to the eighth century, who didn't even have a name until the 1400s. In Japan, his story is just as well known as the tales of Momotarō and Kintarō (see their entries), but it is different in its strange twist and ultimately sad ending. Unlike the Peach Boy or the Golden Boy, Urashima Tarō wasn't a wunderkind who was born extraordinarily powerful and took part in a lot of epic battles—he was just a normal guy who did a good deed and got rewarded, and then what felt like the right decision landed him in an unfortunate place (you'll read more about this later in the entry).

There are quite a few variations of Urashima Tarō's tale through the ages, many of them quite old. One very ancient reference to his legend can be found at a shrine in northern Kyoto Prefecture called Urashima Jinja (Urashima Shrine). It boasts a document that describes a man named Urashimako who left his land in C.E. 478, went to a place where people never die, and then came back in C.E. 825. Upon returning, Urashimako was carrying an important part of the story, a tamatebako, with him. *Tamatebako* (玉手箱) is a word that was created by combining *tama*, which means "jewel" but has the nuance of meaning "beautiful," with *tebako*, a traditional small box for storing things. Ten days after his return, he opened the beautiful jeweled box, white smoke poured out, and he transformed into an old man who died soon after. Upon hearing this story, the emperor at the time (Emperor Junna) ordered a shrine built to pay homage to both the tamatebako and Urashimako's no doubt disgruntled spirit.

Background and Popular Stories

Otogizōshi (御伽草子), or companion tales, are a group of thirty- to forty-page short stories written and illustrated during the Muromachi era (1336–1573). The authors and artists are mostly unknown, but what is known is that unlike past literary works that came from the aristocracy, these stories were created by a much broader spectrum of society, including monks, hermits, those in the warrior class, and possibly merchants. Scholars debate whether there are only twenty-three "true" otogizōshi or as many as five hundred. Within the authenticated twenty-three tales lies one about Urashima Tarō.

One version of his fairy tale goes like this. Long ago, a young fisherman saw some rambunctious boys hitting a sea turtle with sticks. He shooed the children away, saving the poor animal. The next day, the turtle returned and told him as a reward for saving its life, the dragon god (see the Ryū entry) had invited him for a visit to his dragon palace, Ryūgū-jō. Urashima Tarō accepted; he climbed on the turtle's back and off they went.

There he was met by Otohime (乙姫) (the grandmother of Japan's first emperor, Jimmu), the dragon god's daughter. They spent three days enjoying each other's company in the magical underwater palace made of coral and gold and silver. On day three, however, Urashima Tarō suddenly had the urge to see his aging mother again. He told this to Otohime, saying he wished to return home.

She was saddened to hear his decision but understood his feelings. Oto-hime then presented him with a tamatebako as a parting gift and told him to take it with him but to never open it. He agreed, climbed back on the turtle, and departed the magnificent dragon palace forever.

After arriving home, though, Urashima Tarō noticed that everything looked different than he remembered. His mother's house was gone and even more disturbing, no one knew who he was. He retraced his steps to the beach and encountered a very elderly man who had heard the name Urashima Tarō. However, the old man recounted that Urashima Tarō was a figure of legends who'd disappeared from that very shore before the old man was even born.

As it turned out, three hundred years had passed since Urashima Tarō had first taken a ride on that fateful turtle and visited the Ryūgū-jō.

The realization that everything he knew was gone, and that a return to the dragon palace again was impossible, thoroughly depressed the young fisherman. He sat down and—whether intentionally or unintentionally, no one will ever know—he opened the tamatebako that he'd vowed to keep sealed. In an instant, he was engulfed in white smoke and transformed into a very old man with a long white beard and hair.

Some early variations of the tale have him going instead to a mountain called Hōrai or Tokoyo no kuni (meaning "Timeless Land"). Mount Hōrai in Chinese mythology is called Mount Penglai and believed to be a legend-ary, magical place where all the animals were pure white, and jewels and enchanted fruits grew on trees. This fruit could cure any disease, grant eternal youth, and bring back the dead. Immortals lived in palaces made of gold, silver, and platinum, and from the top of the Mount Hōrai billowed the smoke of the burning elixir of immortality.

In Modern Stories

Urashima Tarō is indeed ageless, while maybe not quite as prevalent in modern culture as Kintarō and Momotarō. Still, you can find mention of him in author Ursula K. Le Guin's short story "Another Story, or A Fisherman of the Inland Sea" as well as in the manga and anime *Gintama* in the Ryūgūjō arc, which has the turtle, Ryūgū Palace, Otohime, and Urashima, who ends up sealed in a cryo-chamber. There is also a "bad" version of the folk hero named Ura Urashima (which translates to "Reverse Urashima") in the manga series *YuYu Hakusho*.

NOW YOU KNOW

Urashima Tarō's story is so uniquely captivating that it has sparked some interesting interpretations. There are people who speculate the turtle—with its domed shape—was actually an alien saucer-shaped UAP (unidentified autonomous phenomenon). The children's attacks with sticks were attempts to gain entry. The theory goes on to suggest his journey was into outer space, where rapid travel preserved his youth. Alternately, some view it as a time machine story, or just an incredibly early science fiction tale.

USHIONI

牛鬼

Pronunciation: OO-shee-OH-nee

Translation: Ox Demon, Bull Demon

Also known as: Gyūki (牛鬼), the same characters,
but pronounced GYOO-kee

Overview

Ushioni are large, vicious, and ultimately deadly yōkai that have a couple of different manifestations. On one hand, they can look like what their name implies, an ox head on an oni (demon) body or, rarer, an ox head on a kimono-clad human body. But more often than not, in old scrolls and artwork, this cow demon appears bafflingly as a giant six-legged spider with bladed claws and an ox's head. In this second manifestation, the ushioni also have soft bodies, bright red horns, long tongues, and fangs. It's said that despite being so huge, they are utterly silent when sneaking up behind you.

To further add to the incongruity of the creatures, these giant cow spiders are associated with water and are mostly found along the western coasts of Japan and Shikoku as well as deep in the mountains near lakes and rivers, and in swamps and waterfalls.

If you're ever out hiking in the mountains, keep an eye on deep pools of water. If they are muddied, or worse, you see some whiskers or a tail sticking up above the surface, that's a sure sign an ushioni lives there.

Sometimes they've been known to transform into beautiful women, which can be confusing as well. But don't worry—if you ever meet a random radiant lady standing beside a lake in the middle of a forest, stay calm and look at her reflection in the water. It'll reveal her true form.

Background and Popular Stories

The ushioni have been written about a lot through the ages. One early example is the Heian-era (C.E. 794–1185) work *Makura no Sōshi* (枕草子), *The Pillow Book*, where it was referred to as an "osoroshiki mono" or "terrible thing."

How terrible? Well, ushioni will unapologetically eat you alive and on top of that are virtually impossible to defeat. If you fight them off and manage to escape, they won't forget, and sometime in your future, when you least expect it, they will find you and then devour you whole.

You're not off the hook if you just *see* one either. Merely glimpsing an ushioni will make you sick, sometimes to the point of vomiting blood. Reportedly, some ushioni can spew poison from vast distances. So much for running. Then there is the mind-boggling technique the ushioni in Wakayama Prefecture employ: If one licks your shadow, you will fall ill with a fever and possibly die. It's called "kage wo kū," or "eating your shadow." They are, in effect, eating your soul.

There's a temple in Kagawa Prefecture called Negorōji, which means "fragrant camellia root," that has a special relationship with the ushioni. The legend goes that about four hundred years ago, an ushioni appeared near the temple and destroyed the fields. A master archer named Yamada Kurando Takakiyo was called to dispatch the fiend. But no matter how many days Takakiyo waited, it didn't return. The archer then prayed to the deity of the temple, Senju Kannon, asking for help to flush out the ushioni.

Finally, on the twenty-first day, Takakiyo saw the sparkle of the beast's eyes across the field, and he shot. His first arrow missed. He shot again.

His second arrow missed. But the third arrow struck the ushioni in its open mouth. The mythical monster howled in pain and ran off.

Takakiyo followed the blood trail until he came across its dead body. He cut off the horns, brought them to the temple, and presented them to the head monk. It's said to this day the ushioni's horns are still housed at the Negorōji Temple in a wooden box labeled "Ushioni."

Also on display at the temple is a statue of what that particular ushioni looked like. It's weirdly adorable and an unusual variation; it has a monkey-like head, ox horns, big round eyes, and bat-like ears. It's standing upright on two legs and its open mouth reveals downward-pointing fangs. It also has the striped furry body of a tiger and frilled bat wings under its arms.

Another peculiar detail about the ox demon is that there have always been rumors that this brutal beast is actually the spirit of a camellia root. (Remember, the temple in the story's name actually means "fragrant camellia root.") Camellia is called tsubaki in Japanese, and it is considered an important and holy flower that contains a great spirit. For some reason, they are often found in places where an ushioni appears.

The following legend explains the possible connection between tsubaki and ushioni. One night a long time ago, an old fisherman went out to sea to fish. While on the dark water, he saw an ushioni and bravely attacked it. He then dragged the body all the way back to his home, where he left it in front of his house and fell promptly asleep from exhaustion.

The next day, he called all the villagers to brag about his accomplishment. No one had ever beaten an ushioni before. Everyone gathered around to see this loathsome beast he'd killed with his bare hands. After a few minutes, one of the villagers went over and struck it with a stick. He then announced that the old man must be half-blind. It wasn't an ushioni, but just a large old tsubaki root.

In Modern Stories

The ushioni is no stranger to modern times. Going by its other name, gyūki, it shows up in the manga and anime *Naruto*, but instead of appearing as a spider, it's half-octopus. It's also featured in the game *Nioh 2* as the giant spider beast.

> ### NOW YOU KNOW
>
> Despite their reputation as human-flesh-rending monsters, there's at least one tale that shows ushioni in a kinder light. Long ago, a young man in Wakayama Prefecture named Ueda shared some of his food with a hungry woman he met by the Mio River. Two months later, while he was walking by the same area, a sudden flash flood swept him away. Drowning, he looked toward the shore and saw the woman he'd shared food with. She quickly transformed into an ushioni, swam out, and saved his life. Sadly, though, when an ushioni saves a human, their body melts away and they disappear.

YAMAUBA
山姥

Pronunciation: YAH-mah-OO-bah

Translation: Mountain Witch or Mountain Crone

Also known as: Yamanba (山姥), Onibaba (鬼婆),
Yamahime (山姫), Yamaonna (山女), Kijo (鬼女)

Overview

Yamauba are mountain-dwelling yōkai that resemble dreadful old hags. These mountain witches, for the most part, wear filthy, tattered kimonos or skirts made of tree bark and have darkly tanned and deeply wrinkled skin. Their red or stark white hair is long and tangled and is sometimes tied back with a piece of straw. When one is chasing her prey at inhuman speeds, though, her eyes flash blue, her mouth stretches from ear to ear, and those uncombed locks stand out in all directions.

Yamauba live in rickety huts or in caves and are rumored to be real women who have left their homes or were banished for one reason or another. Over time, their circumstances—together with a hefty dose of bitterness and resentment—apparently turn them into these cannibalistic supernatural monsters.

There are actually two types of yamauba. One will chase you down and chop you up or, if really hungry, eat you alive. These flesh-eating kind do things like snatch children away from their parents and target anyone walking alone in mountain passes. If you are lost or the weather is turning bad, a yamauba might appear a little more well-groomed and kindly offer you a place to stay for the night, where you will no doubt meet your grisly end.

The second variety, though, is quite the opposite in character. She'll venture down into villages and rice fields and dispense good luck and fortune. This more compassionate mountain witch is portrayed as a maternal figure and can be seen in the legend of Kintarō (see his earlier entry), where his mother, a yamauba on Mount Ashigara, cares for the young hero and raises him lovingly.

There are also tales of people running across these beneficent yamauba going into labor. The concerned person helps out and ends up delivering thousands of the yamauba's babies. Their diligence and (no doubt) trauma are thusly rewarded when afterward they are blessed with great wealth and prosperity.

Sadly, another way to gain fortune with a mountain crone is to capture and burn her. Legend says her body will turn into all sorts of lucky items, like gold, silver, medicine, rice, millet, silk, and even silkworms.

Background and Popular Stories

A very popular children's story about a yamauba is called "Sanmai no Ofuda" or "The Three Charms and the Mountain Witch." Once, there was a young, mischievous apprentice monk who lived in a temple in the mountains. He was always taking naps and playing pranks and never listening to the head monk. One autumn day, the boy saw that the chestnut trees higher up in the mountains were starting to bear fruit and asked if he could go collect some.

The head monk told him it was very dangerous, as a wicked yamauba lived near there and would eat him up. But the young boy laughed and said he didn't believe in such things and begged to be allowed to go. This went on until the head monk finally decided such an experience might teach the young boy a lesson and gave him permission. He presented the boy with three paper ofuda (お札) charms (sacred amulets believed to possess spiritual power and offer protection) and told him to use them wisely.

The apprentice climbed into the hills and began filling a bag with chestnuts. He lost track of time and soon noticed it was getting dark. He was about to hurry back to the temple when he heard a woman's voice behind him.

"Look! A young boy!"

The little monk was afraid it was the yamauba, but when he turned there was only a kindly old woman standing there. She said it was probably too dangerous to go home at this late hour and suggested he stay with her for the night in her little house. She offered to roast the chestnuts for him. The hungry boy agreed, and he ate so many of the delicious nuts that he fell asleep on the floor. When he woke up, it was late, and he was alone in the room. He heard a strange sound coming from next door and peeked in. There sitting on the floor was the old woman—only she had changed into a scary hag and was sharpening a large knife.

She sprang across the room and grabbed him before he could even turn to run. Cackling, she said that she intended to eat him up. The apprentice monk said that he understood that, but the whole shock of the situation made him really have to go to the outhouse. He'd be right back.

The yamauba was no fool. She tied a long rope around his waist and, clutching one end in her hand, let him out the front door. The boy went into the outhouse and tried to think of a plan. It wasn't long before she called out, "Are you finished yet?"

"Not yet," the boy replied. This went on a couple of times until he suddenly remembered the three ofuda charms. He pulled one out and stuck it to the door, praying to it. He implored, "Please, pretend to be me and answer her when she calls." With that, he untied the rope and snuck out a back window.

"Are you done yet?" the witch shouted again.

"Not yet!" This time it was the ofuda talking.

This back and forth continued until the yamauba realized something was wrong. She threw open the door and found her young meal gone. The boy monk had gotten a head start, but the mountain witch was very fast. She screeched as she ran after him, gaining quickly.

The boy grabbed the second ofuda and prayed for a large river to be made between them. *Whoosh!* It happened, washing over the frightening hag. But before the boy could get too confident, the yamauba swallowed up all the water and continued her chase.

He could see the temple but still wasn't close enough to be safe. He pulled out the last ofuda and this time wished for a sea of fire to spring up behind him. *Whoosh!* A sea of fire appeared. But the yamauba spit out all the water she had just swallowed and extinguished the fire. The terrified boy barely made it into the temple's main hall to find the head monk sitting on the floor, roasting rice cakes over a fire. Without words he understood what was going on and hid the boy inside a large vase.

The yamauba burst into the room and demanded the boy. The head monk said he didn't know anything about that but suggested they have a test of powers. If she won, he would sacrifice himself for her evening meal. The mountain witch agreed.

The monk asked her to make herself huge. The old hag laughed and turned herself into a giant. The monk agreed that was impressive and then asked her to make herself as small as a bean. She immediately turned herself tiny.

"Now it's my turn," said the head monk, and he plucked her up, stuffed her into a rice cake, and popped her in his mouth and swallowed.

The wicked mountain witch was never seen again, and the little apprentice monk became a very good listener and a very hard worker.

In Modern Stories

There is a yamauba character in the Bushido: Cult of Yurei board game. She also appears as a powerful knife-wielding enemy in the game *Nioh 2* and as a spiky-haired old lady in products from the Japanese media franchise *Yo-kai Watch*. In folktales about Kintarō, his mother is usually portrayed as a yamauba.

NOW YOU KNOW

In the mid-1990s, there was a fashion trend started in Shibuya and Ikebukuro called ganguro (顔黒). It involved getting dark tans and using white concealer for lipstick and eyeshadow. Later, the more extreme "yamanba" style appeared. These very tanned teens with their wild colorful wigs and extensions were thought to resemble the mythical mountain witch, hence the name.

YATAGARASU

八咫烏

Pronunciation: YAH-tah-GAH-rah-soo

Translation: Eight-Span Crow or Raven

Etymology: The first character means "eight," the second in this case just means "very large," and the third means "crow." So, a crow that is "very large" times eight.

Overview

The yatagarasu is an incarnation of a mythical Shinto kami (god) that was sent from heaven to guide Japan's first emperor, Jimmu, on his eastern expedition from Kumano through the mountains to Yamato. It looks like an enormous crow and is called the god of guidance.

This holy bird was written about in both the *Kojiki* (C.E. 712) and the *Nihon Shoki* (C.E. 720), although the stories differ somewhat. One thing that wasn't mentioned in either of those classic books but sets it apart from other large crows is that the yatagarasu has three legs. This curious trait seems to have popped up later in the Heian era (C.E. 794–1185).

If you look back at Chinese and Korean mythology, you'll also find a three-legged crow. Since some stories, religion, and culture were brought to Japan from China and Korea throughout the years, it's most likely those three-legged crow legends merged with Japan's mythological bird, giving us the yatagarasu we have today.

Both the Chinese and Japanese myths associate this fabled crow with the sun, but one difference is that in Chinese mythology, the deity is believed to live *in* the sun (maybe due to the observance of sunspots by ancient astronomers), while in Japanese mythology the yatagarasu is an incarnation *of* the sun.

Why three legs? The Kumano Hongu Taisha Shrine in Wakayama Prefecture says that the three legs represent heaven, Earth, and humankind. They could also represent the three Kumano clans that once controlled the region (the Ui, Suzuki, and Enomoto). According to Chinese thought, though, the legs stand for sunrise, daylight, and sunset.

Background and Popular Stories

In Kyoto, along the Kamo River, there is a sprawling Shinto sanctuary complex that includes a pair of shrines that are the most important and oldest in the city. They are the Kamigamo Jinja (上賀茂神社), or Upper Kamo Shrine, and the Shimogamo Jinja (下鴨神社), or Lower Kamo Shrine. Together, they are called the Kamo Shrines.

While there are numerous deities enshrined throughout this complex, the one we'll talk about here is Kamo Wakeikazuchi. That myth goes something like this.

Once upon a time, the god Kamo Taketsunumi no Mikoto descended from heaven to Mount Mikage, where it appeared as a three-legged crow deity of the sun, the yatagarasu. While in this form, the deity led Emperor Jimmu throughout Kyoto to the plains of Yamato, which is where the emperor then founded what would later become the Japanese nation. It was also there that the Shimogamo Jinja would eventually be built.

Kamo Taketsunumi no Mikoto had a daughter, Tamayori Hime who one day, while bathing in the Kamo River, encountered a red arrow that transformed into the dashing Honoikazuchi, the god of fire and thunder. The two married and had a son—also a thunder god—named Kamo Wakeikazuchi.

The Kamigamo Jinja shrine is dedicated to Kamo Wakeikazuchi, who is believed to control lightning, thunder, and natural disasters. The second shrine, Shimogamo Jinja venerates Tamayori Hime (his mother) and Kamo Taketsunumi no Mikoto (her father, the original three-legged crow).

In Modern Stories

Yatagarasu Attack on Cataclysm is a doujin fighting game, kind of like the *Street Fighter* games. Then there is the anime *Noragami*, which has a three-legged crow god named Yatagarasu, and an Onmyōdo card game that features the yatagarasu. There is also a fantasy series called Yatagarasu: The Legendary Birds by author Chisato Abe.

There's even a manga/anime called *Yata Garasu* about a soccer player, for whom three legs might come in handy. This also seems fitting when you consider that the Japan Football Association uses the yatagarasu in its logo. One of its three legs is holding a soccer ball.

YUKI ONNA
雪女

Pronunciation: YOO-key OH-nah

Translation: Snow Woman

Also known as: Yuki Musume (雪娘), Snow Daughter;
Yuki Jorō (雪女郎), Snow Harlot; Yukifuri Baba (雪降り婆),
Snowfall Hag; Tsurara Onna (氷柱女), Icicle Woman

Overview

Yuki onna, or the snow woman, is an ancient ethereal beauty whose tale has been passed down for generations and whose ghostly presence has made it into the yōkai canon. She is known by many different names and is included in at least as many legends. Not only is she depicted in Toriyama Sekien's first collection, *Gazu Hyakki Yagyō* (画図百鬼夜行), or *Illustrated Demon Horde's Night Parade* (1776), but she appears in a black-and-white image as a barefoot giantess in an even earlier work called the *Sōgi Shokoku Monogatari* (1685).

The snow woman appears on wintry nights as a tall—sometimes more than 10 feet (3 meters)!—bewitching beauty with blue lips, translucent skin that's colder than ice, and long black hair blowing in the wind. She seemingly floats across the snow toward you, leaving no footprints. Because Japanese ghosts are noted for their absence of feet, it makes you wonder if she is one.

Another clue that she started out as more of a specter is that she can turn herself into a cloud of mist or snow and vanish at will, especially if she feels threatened. According to some, she's actually the ghost of someone who died in the snow and returned from the dead. Then there are those who believe she's a spirit of the snow.

There are hundreds of variations of this wintry maiden—but whatever the story, those who come across her or hear her knocking at their door are apt to die, usually by freezing to death.

Background and Popular Stories

Lafcadio Hearn's tale "Yuki-Onna" is probably the best-known story of this femme fatale. Long ago, there lived two woodcutters: an old man named Mosaku and his eighteen-year-old apprentice, Minokichi. Every day they traveled to a distant forest on the other side of a wide river, where they worked. As there were no bridges, the only way to cross the river was by ferry.

Late one day after work, they were on their way home when they noticed a snowstorm approaching. The two spotted the ferry on the far shore, but the boatman was nowhere to be seen. Stranded, they decided to take shelter in the ferryman's tiny hut to spend the night and weather the blizzard. They had no fire but curled up and covered themselves in their straw mino coats and tried to sleep. The older Mosaku fell asleep quickly, while Minokichi listened to the gales outside shake the walls and shivered as the temperatures continued to fall. After some time, he, too, found sleep.

Suddenly, Minokichi was awakened by a sprinkling of snow on his face. He noticed the door had been blown open, and a beautiful woman in all white with frightening eyes was standing in the room. She bent down over him and whispered in his ear that she had intended to do the same thing to him as she'd done to Mosaku, but because he was young and good-looking, she'd spare him. But she'd only do that if he promised to never tell anyone about meeting her. If he said anything, she would know and would kill him.

Minokichi survived the encounter and the night, but his mentor, Mosaku, didn't. The younger man returned home quite shaken by the whole experience but, keeping his word, told no one about what had happened or the beautiful and terrifying snow woman.

A year or so later, Minokichi was walking home and ran into a woman he'd never met before. Her name was Oyuki (which means "snow") and, long story short, the two fell in love and soon wed. The couple were happy and had ten children, all of whom were very good-looking and had incredibly fair skin. The entire town adored Oyuki, and it was remarkable how even after having so many babies, she never seemed to age. Life was pure bliss until, one night, when Minokichi was home watching his wife sew by candlelight and became overcome with emotion. Without thinking, he said she reminded him of someone he had met many years ago. Oyuki asked who that was, and Minokichi told of the incident in the hut the night Mosaku had died. He added that, even today, he wasn't sure if it had just been a dream.

Without warning, Oyuki threw down her sewing and flew across the room. She stood over her husband, shrieking. She said it had been she who had visited him in the hut that night. But now he had broken his promise, and she should end his life right then and there. But Oyuki paused and looked toward the room where their children slept. She made him promise to take very good care of them and told him that if any one of them ever had a complaint about him, she'd return and kill him immediately.

She began to scream, her voice growing thin until it sounded like the whistling wind. At the same time, right before his eyes, his wife's body melted away into a bright white mist that disappeared through the smoke hole. She was never seen again.

In Modern Stories

The Ice Apparitions (kōrime) in the manga and anime *YuYu Hakusho* were inspired by the yuki onna, as were the Pokémon Froslass and the character Frostina from *Yo-kai Watch*.

Akira Kurosawa's 1990 film *Dreams* also has an appearance of the yuki onna in the part titled "The Blizzard."

ZASHIKI WARASHI
座敷童 or 座敷童子

Pronunciation: ZAH-shee-key WAH-rah-shee

Translation: The Guest-Room Child, the Parlor-Room Child, (literally) Room Child

Etymology: A *zashiki* is a tatami mat (or wooden) floored guest room found in traditional Japanese homes. *Warashi* is an old word that means child.

Also known as: Zashiki Bokko (座敷ぼっこ), Zashiki Warabe (座敷童), Zashiki Kozō (座敷小僧)

Overview

If you're lucky enough to catch sight of a zashiki warashi, you'll find it looks like a ghostly child with a bob haircut and bangs, or a completely shaven head. They wear traditional clothing, like a chanchanko jacket (a padded vest, sometimes sleeveless—like the one worn by Kitarō in *GeGeGe no Kitarō*) and a kimono that can be either formal or extremely humble. Their outfits are usually dark in tone with traditional designs, although red is also reported. These otherworldly children appear to be from an older age. Judging from artwork and descriptions from firsthand witnesses, they can be either super cute or super scary.

The zashiki warashi is another yōkai that prefers to be elusive, not often showing its real form but instead choosing to cause mischief and play harmless little tricks about the house. It might walk around or make rustling noises in rooms no one is supposed to be in, leave little footprints on the floor, turn over pillows, and touch or climb on top of people while they sleep.

Creepiness aside, zashiki warashi are considered lucky. To have one residing in your house will bring prosperity and all good things to you and your family. It is quite the opposite of cohabitating with a binbōgami, or poverty god (see the Binbōgami entry), who just wants to make your life miserable. Because of this, all those strange occurrences—the pranks, the being stepped on in the middle of the night—should be welcomed, and the zashiki warashi should be treated like the honored guest they are. Some families go as far as to offer them daily small meals of sekihan, red beans mixed with mochi rice, a lucky dish for a lucky yōkai.

Background and Popular Stories

Zashiki warashi are commonly associated with the Tōhoku, or northeast, area of Japan, with Iwate Prefecture being particularly well known for them. There's even an inn called Ryokufusō (緑風荘) in Ninohe City that is famous for zashiki warashi sightings and other paranormal experiences associated with these yōkai. The story goes that 670 years ago, the owner of Ryokufusō's ancestor traveled all the way from an area around present-day Tokyo to where the inn is currently located. On the way, his oldest son Kamemaro—who was six years old at the time—suddenly collapsed and died. The boy's last words were, "I will protect my family until the end of time."

True to his word, the boy became a guardian spirit of the hotel and is said to occasionally appear in the room called Enjū no Ma. Some of the guests who have seen him in his zashiki warashi form or experienced something strange at the inn have returned home and attained great fortune or career advancements or found the perfect spouse. As you might guess, staying at the inn is extremely popular, and occasionally there is a waiting list years long to book a room.

On October 4, 2009, however, a fire broke out and burned the entire place down. This might sound like a very unlucky occurrence, but the staff say there were thirty or so people staying in the hotel that night, and miraculously everyone escaped unharmed. Also, a nearby shrine that was dedicated to the zashiki warashi completely escaped any damage. They believe the zashiki warashi helped everyone escape, then stayed at the shrine until the hotel was rebuilt. Once it was reopened, the guardian spirit returned to help it gain prosperity again.

Less common is another kind of house spirit somewhat related to the zashiki warashi called the hosode (細手) (meaning skinny arms) or hosode-nagate (細手長手) (meaning skinny long arms). This yōkai, too, frequently visits sleeping individuals. Only, instead of a child giggling and moving your pillow around, during the night, a pair of absurdly long, slender arms belonging to a child reaches out across the room to shake you awake.

Why do hosode-nagate wake people up? The consensus is mixed on this one. Some recounts tell of misfortune befalling the person who was awakened by the hosode-nagate—like one man who, after being beckoned by a pair of long skinny arms from the back of a room, lost his wife shortly after in a tsunami. Another man lost his house after a similar incident when the river overflowed and carried it away.

Conversely, there are other tales of hosode-nagate's arms moving around the tatami mat floor like vines to rouse a sleeper. But this time it is to warn them of an upcoming disaster, perhaps a tsunami or a flood.

In Modern Stories

Zashiki Warashi no Tatami Chan is an anime that features a lead character zashiki warashi. But they also show up as both the gnome-looking Gnomey and the charming young adult Zashiki Warashi in *Yo-kai Watch*, then as a lovely young woman in the manga and anime *xxxHOLiC*, and again with their weird and colorful depictions in the animated series *Mononoke*.

FURTHER READING

Foster, Michael Dylan. *The Book of Yōkai: Mysterious Creatures of Japanese Folklore*. Oakland, CA: University of California Press, 2015.

Foster, Michael Dylan. *Pandemonium and Parade: Japanese Monsters and the Culture of Yōkai*. Berkeley, CA: University of California Press, 2009.

Hearn, Lafcadio. *Exotics and Retrospectives*. Project Gutenberg, 2013. www.gutenberg.org/ebooks/42735

Hearn, Lafcadio. *Gleanings in Buddha-Fields: Studies of Hand and Soul in the Far East*. Project Gutenberg, 2017. www.gutenberg.org/ebooks/55681

Hearn, Lafcadio. *Glimpses of Unfamiliar Japan*. Project Gutenberg, 2005. www.gutenberg.org/ebooks/8130

Hearn, Lafcadio. *In Ghostly Japan*. Project Gutenberg, 2005. www.gutenberg.org/ebooks/8128

Hearn, Lafcadio. *Japan: An Attempt at Interpretation*. Project Gutenberg, 2004. www.gutenberg.org/ebooks/5979

Hearn, Lafcadio. *Kokoro: Hints and Echoes of Japanese Inner Life*. Project Gutenberg, 2005. www.gutenberg.org/ebooks/8882

Hearn, Lafcadio. *Kwaidan: Stories and Studies of Strange Things.* Project Gutenberg, 1998. www.gutenberg.org/ebooks/1210

Hearn, Lafcadio. *Shadowings.* Project Gutenberg, 2010. www.gutenberg.org/ebooks/34215

Ito, Nobukazu. *Yokai.* Tokyo, Japan: PIE International, 2021.

Kawai, Hayao. *Dreams, Myths & Fairy Tales in Japan.* Einsiedeln, Switzerland: Daimon, 2012.

Kazuhiko, Komatsu. *An Introduction to Yōkai Culture: Monsters, Ghosts, and Outsiders in Japanese History.* Translated by Hiroko Yoda and Matt Alt. Tokyo, Japan: Japan Publishing Industry Foundation for Culture, 2017.

Kunio, Yanagita. *The Legends of Tono, 100th Anniversary Edition.* Translated by Ronald A. Morse. Lanham, MD: Lexington Books, 1955.

Masao, Higashi. Kaiki: *Uncanny Tales from Japan, Volume 1: Tales of Old Edo.* Kumamoto, Japan: Kurodahan Press, 2009.

Mayer, Fanny Hagin, ed. *The Yanagita Kunio Guide to the Japanese Folk Tale.* Bloomington, IN: Indiana University Press, 1986.

Yoda, Hiroko and Matt Alt, trans. *Japandemonium Illustrated: The Yokai Encyclopedias of Toriyama Sekien.* New York: Dover Publications, 2017.

Yoda, Hiroko and Matt Alt. *Yokai Attack! The Japanese Monster Survival Guide.* Rutland, VT: Tuttle Publishing, 2012.

GLOSSARY

These are some of the more common words, phrases, and people that you'll hear about when studying Japanese folklore, yōkai, and mythical heroes.

bō (坊):

An endearing suffix used sometimes after a boy's name. The character for *bō* literally means "monk." It is also found in the words *bōya* (坊や), *botchan* (坊つちゃん), and *bōzu* (坊主). These are all terms used to refer to young boys. They can be affectionate expressions or, depending on the usage, have a more negative, demeaning nuance.

Buddhism:

A major world religion and philosophical system that originated in ancient India around the fifth century B.C.E. It's based on the teachings of Siddhartha Gautama, known as the Buddha, who sought to understand the nature of suffering and the path to liberation from it. Buddhism was introduced to Japan in the sixth century C.E. Over time, Japanese Buddhism has developed distinct traditions and schools, sometimes incorporating Indigenous beliefs and practices. Buddhism in Japan coexists alongside Shinto, and many Japanese people observe both traditions. Buddhist temples are called otera (お寺).

kami (神):

Literally means "god," but in the Shinto religion, it refers to deities, spirits, or ancestral or otherwise spiritual entities that embody various natural elements. In the Ainu (Indigenous people of Hokkaido) language, *kamuy* is a similar concept.

Kojiki (古事記):

Translated as *The Record of Ancient Matters* in English, the *Kojiki* (C.E. 712) is a chronicle of Japanese myths, legends, songs, poems, and semihistorical accounts. It is considered the oldest extant literary work in Japan.

kozō (小僧):

The characters for *kozō*, similar to *bō*, literally mean "small monk," and that's what it used to mean ages ago. A kozō was a young monk or acolyte studying and training at a temple. But it also has a second meaning when used to refer to any young boy or young man, kind of like "youngster," "kid," or "lad." But *kozō* is tricky in that it can also have a derogatory feel to it. You'll often find it as a suffix on a name or nickname from old Japan (see the Hitotsume Kozō and Tōfu Kozō entries). *Kozō* is still used today and is still a very nuanced word. Depending on the intonation and use, *kozō* can be highly offensive, lightly teasing, or even affectionate.

Lafcadio Hearn (1850–1904):

A Greek Japanese writer, translator, and teacher. Later in life, in 1890, Hearn traveled to Japan as a newspaper correspondent, but ended up remaining there for the rest of his life. He married a Japanese national (named Setsuko) and took a Japanese name, Koizumi Yakumo (小泉八雲). Hearn traveled around Japan and collected stories, which he retold in English. These stories were then translated back into Japanese and enjoyed once more. His Japanese-related works are listed in the Further Reading section. They can be found and read for free on Project Gutenberg.

Mizuki Shigeru (水木しげる) (1922–2015):

A highly renowned Japanese manga artist and author. He's best known for creating the beloved *GeGeGe no Kitarō* series, which debuted in 1960 and follows the adventures of Kitarō along with his yōkai friends.

Nihon Shoki (日本書紀):

This C.E. 720 work is translated in English as *The Chronicles of Japan*. Commissioned by Emperor Tenmu and compiled by a team of scholars, it is considered one of the oldest extant chronicles of Japanese history. It records the mythological creation of Japan all the way to the eighth century, giving great insights into ancient Japanese society, culture, and religious beliefs.

ofuda (お札):

A type of talisman or amulet sold at Japanese temples and shrines.

oni (鬼):

This fearsome, mythical, ogre-like creature appears in Japanese art, literature, and folktales throughout the ages. While there are some stories of kinder oni, most are bloodthirsty brutes who embody and symbolize all the more sinister and dreadful elements of life.

otogizōshi (御伽草子):

Also called companion tales, these are a group of thirty- to forty-page-length short stories written and illustrated during the Muromachi era (1336–1573). The authors and artists are mostly unknown, but what is known is that unlike past literary works that came from the aristocracy, these stories were created by a much broader spectrum of society including monks, hermits, those in the warrior class, and possibly merchants.

Shinto:

The Indigenous religion of Japan that focuses on the worship of deities, spirits, and nature. One of Shinto's essential beliefs is that of kami (gods or divine or sacred spirits). Kami are believed to inhabit not only natural elements, like mountains, trees, and rivers, but also other inanimate objects.

Toriyama Sekien (鳥山石燕) (1712–1788):

Not only a master artist and learned scholar, this prolific storyteller was also very adept at wordplay and puns. The phrase he used in the title of the first of his four popular books, *hyakki yagyō* (百鬼夜行), literally means "one hundred oni night parade," but it's also an idiom meaning "pandemonium" and gives the image of an uncountable horde.

Wakan Sansai Zue (和漢三才図会):

Translated as *Illustrated Sino-Japanese Encyclopedia* and compiled by scholar and doctor Terajima Ryōan, this is an encyclopedia that was published in 1712 (during the Edo era). It consists of multiple volumes and covers a wide range of subjects including natural history, geography, human anatomy, mythology, and more. It inspired Toriyama Sekien.

Yanagita Kunio (柳田國男) (1875–1962):

A Japanese scholar, author, and folklorist who has been labeled the father of modern Japanese folklore. He published many works on folklore and popular religious beliefs, but his 1910 book *Tōno Monogatari* (遠野物語), or *The Legends of Tono*, has become a Japanese and folklore classic.

INDEX

A

Abe no Seimei, 19–23, 67

Akaname, 25–27

Amabie (aka amabiko), 28–33

Animals, patchwork of numerous (baku), 43–47

Azukiarai, 34–37

B

Bō, defined, 232

Baby, old man who cries like (Konaki Jiji), 115–18

Bakeneko and nekomata, 39–42

Baku, 43–47

Bathtub dirt, yōkai to clean. See Akaname

Bean washer (azukiarai), 34–37

Binbōgami, 49–52

Boat ghosts (funayūrei), 202

Bride, entangling (jorōgumo), 87–90

Bridge maiden/princess (Hashihime), 65–68

Buddhism, defined, 232–33

Bull demon (ushioni), 207–11

C

Cat with fish body, 80–81

Cat yōkai (bakeneko and nekomata), 39–42

Child, guest-room/parlor-room (zashiki warashi), 227–29

Child of the mallet/hammer (tsuchinoko), 191–95

Cloth, on length of cotton. See Ittan momen

COVID-19, 28

Crow/raven, eight-span (yatagarasu), 218–20

D

Demon fires and fox fires (onibi and kitsunebi), 150–53

Demon/ogre (oni), 145–49

Dog, heavenly (tengu), 177–81

Dog, racoon (tanuki), 177–81

Dorotabō, 53–57

Dragon (ryū), 167–71

Dragon god (Ryūjin), 31, 127, 170

Dream eater (baku), 43–47

E

Earth/dirt spider (tsuchigumo), 187–90

Entangling bride (jorōgumo), 87–90

F

Faceless human (nopperabō), 129–33

Fish, human (ningyo), 125–28

Five Elements, Theory of, 19–20

Fūjin and Raijin, 155–58

Flatulence. See Kappa

Flying beast, wingless (nue), 135–38

Foxes (kitsune), 105–10

Fox fires, demon fires and (onibi and kitsunebi), 150–53

Futakuchi onna, 59–63

G

Glossary of terms, 232–35

Golden boy. *See* Kintarō

H

Hammer/mallet, child of (tsuchinoko), 191–95

Harlot spider (jorōgumo), 87–90

Hashihime, 65–68

Hearn, Lafcadio, 46, 130, 133, 164, 222, 233–34

Heavenly dog (tengu), 177–81

Hitotsume kozō, 69–73. *See also* Tōfu Kozō

Human-faced tree/dog/fish (jinmenju/ jinmenken/jinmengyo), 78–81

Human-faced "tumor" (jinmansō), 82–85

I

Ill fotune, bringer of (binbōgami), 49–52

Iris, warding off evil spirits, 63

Ittan momen, 74–77

J

Japanese folklore

about: author's background and perspective, 8–9

additional information/sources, 16–17, 230–31

bad luck causes and, 13

first writings about, 10

names of entities, 14

overlapping stories/legends/ traditions, 15–16

power and mystery of, 13–14

range of entities in, 10–11

terminology and origins of, 14–15

this book and, 11

yōkai and you, 17–18

Jinmenju, jinmenken, and jinmengyo, 78–81

Jinmensō, 82–85

Jorōgumo, 87–90

K

Kamaitachi, 91–94

Kami, definition/overview, 14, 233

Kappa, 95–99

Kintarō, 15–16, 101–4, 118. *See also* Momotaro

Kitsune, 105–10

Kitsunebi, onibi and, 150–53

Kodama, 111–13

Kojiki, 10, 17, 111, 146, 168, 184, 191, 218, 233

Konaki Jiji, 115–18

Kozō, defined, 233

Kunio, Yanagita, 70, 235

Kyūki, 92

L

Lightning and thunder (Fūjin and Raijin), 155–58

Long-necked woman (rokurokubi), 163–66, 184

M

Mallet/hammer, child of (tsuchinoko), 191–95

Merlin of Japan (Abe no Seimei), 19–23

Mermaid (ningyo), 125–28

Modern stories, characters in

Abe No Seimei, 22–23

akaname, 27

amabie (aka amabiko), 32

azukiarai, 37

bakeneko and nekomata, 42
baku, 47
binbōgami, 52
dorotabō, 57
futakuchi onna, 62
Hashihime, 68
hitotsume kozō, 73
ittan momen, 77
jinmansō, 85
jinmenju, jinmenken, jinmengyo, 81
jorōgumo, 90
kamaitachi, 94
kappa, 99
Kintarō, 104
kitsune, 110
kodama, 111–13
Konaki Jiji, 117–18
Momotarō, 121–22
ningyo, 128
nopperabō, 133
nue, 138
ōkami, 143
oni, 145–49
onibi and kitsunebi, 153
raijū, 162
Raijin and Fūjin, 158
rokurokubi, 166
ryū, 171
tōfu kozō, 186
tanuki, 176
tengu, 181
tsuchigumo, 190
tsuchinoko, 195
tsukumogami, 199
umibōzu, 203
Urashima Tarō, 206
ushioni, 211
yamauba, 216

yatagarasu, 220
yuki onna, 225
zashiki warashi, 229
Momotarō, 119–23
Mountain goblin (tengu), 177–81
Mountain witch/crone (yamauba), 213–17
Muddy rice-field goblin (dorotabō), 53–57

N

Nekomata and bakeneko, 39–42
Nightmare eater (baku), 43–47
Nihon Shoki, 10, 17, 96, 111, 130, 173, 184, 191, 218, 234
Ningyo, 125–28
Nopperabō, 129–33
Nue, 135–38

O

Ofuda, 23, 215–16, 234
Ogre/demon (oni), 145–49
Ōkami, 139–43
Old gods/spirits (tsukumogami), 197–99
Old man who cries like baby (Konaki Jiji), 115–18
One-eyed yōkai (dorotabō), 53–57
One-eyed yōkai (hitotsume kozō), 69–73
Oni, 145–49
Oni, defined, 234
Onibi and kitsunebi, 150–53
Onmyōdō/onmyōji, 19–20, 22–23, 146, 147
Otogizōshi, 204, 234–35
Ox demon (ushioni), 207–11

P

Peach boy (Momotarō), 119–23
Pokémon, 42, 47, 57, 62, 81, 94, 99, 113, 158, 162, 181, 195, 225
Poverty god (binbōgami), 49–52
Pranksters. See Hitotsume kozō; Tanuki

R

Racoon dog (tanuki), 173–76
Raijū, 159–62
Raijin and Fūjin, 155–58
Ravenous female yōkai (futakuchi onna), 59–63
Rice-field goblin (dorotabō), 53–57
River child (kappa), 95–99
Rokurokubi, 163–66, 184
Ryū, 167–71
Ryūjin, 31, 127, 170

S

Sea monk (umibōzu), 200–202
"Seimi of Justice" (Abe no Seimei), 19–23
Sekien, Toriyama, about, 235
Shape-shifters, 39, 41, 105–6, 108, 130, 151, 171, 173–74, 180
Shigeru, Mizuki, 28, 75, 117–18, 234
Shinto, defined, 235
Sickle weasel (kamaitachi), 91–94
Snow woman (yuki onna), 221–25
Sources, additional, 16–17, 230–31
Spider, earth/dirt (tsuchigumo), 187–90
Spider, harlot (jorōgumo), 87–90
Squirrel, flying, 76

T

Tōfu kozō (tofu boy), 183–86
Tamamo no Mae, 108–9
Tanuki, 173–76
Tapir-like creature (baku), 43–47
Tarō, Urashima, 203–6
Tengu, 177–81
Thunder and lightning (Raijin and Fūjin), 155–58
Thunder beast/animal (raijū), 159–62
Tree spirit (kodama), 111–13
Tsuchigumo, 187–90

Tsuchinoko, 191–95
Tsukumogami, 197–99
"Tumor," human-faced (jinmensō), 82–85
Two-mouthed woman (futakuchi onna), 59–63

U

Umibōzu, 200–202
Urashima Tarō, 203–6
Ushioni, 207–11

W

Waikan Sansai Zue, 79, 152, 168, 235
Water goblin (kappa), 95–99
Water snake (mizuchi), 96
Weasel, sickle (kamaitachi), 91–94
Wingless flying beast (nue), 135–38
Witch/crone, mountain (yamauba), 213–17
Wolf (ōkami), 139–43

Y

Yōkai. *See also specific entities*
    about: overview of, 14–15
    common folklore sources and, 17
    example, 14–15
    you and, 17–18
Yamauba, 213–17
Yatagarasu, 218–20
Yuki onna, 221–25

Z

Zashiki warashi, 227–29

MORE INCREDIBLE STORIES!

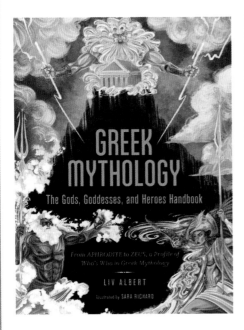

Pick up or download your copies today!

adamsmedia
An Imprint of Simon & Schuster